CAST IRON COOKBOOK
FOR BEGINNERS

Easy Recipes for the Greatest Skillet of All

Clark Allen

Table of Contents

Cook Time: 25 Mins

Total Time: 35 Mins

Prep Time: 10 Mins

Servings: 8

INGREDIENTS

- ½ cup of unsalted butter
- 1 cup of cornmeal
- ½ tsp fine salt
- 1 pinch cayenne pepper
- 3 tbsp honey, or to taste
- 2 large eggs
- ½ cups of buttermilk
- 1 cup of self-rising flour

INSTRUCTIONS

1. Set the oven temperature to 400° Fahrenheit.
2. Dissolve butter in a cast iron skillet. Turn off heat and set butter aside.
3. Mix cornmeal, salt, cayenne pepper, honey, eggs, and buttermilk. To blend the ingredients, whisk them together. Stir in the flour and 1/2 of the butter from the pan. Pour the batter into the skillet with the remaining butter.
4. Finally, bake them for 25 minutes in a preheated oven, or until a toothpick inserted in the middle comes out clean. Allow to cool somewhat before slicing.

NOTES

1. To make your own, combine 1 cup all-purpose flour, 2 tsp baking powder, and 1/2 tsp fine salt in a sifter.

2. You may add spicy peppers, cheese, and fresh corn, as well as change the texture to suit your preferences.
3. I generally use 4 tbsp of butter for the batter and one or two tbsp for the pan, but this time I opted to melt the entire stick. It was on the verge of being too rich, so keep that in mind if you don't want it to be too rich.
4. If you like a super-dry, crumbly cornbread, simply reduce the quantity of buttermilk to 1 cup.

Prep Time: 10 Mins

Cook Time: 25 Mins

Total Time: 35 Mins

Servings: 2

INGREDIENTS

- 2 chicken breasts (about 7 ounce each)
- 1 organic lemon
- A small handful of parsley
- 1 tsp honey
- 2 tbsp divided olive oil
- Fine sea salt and pepper

INSTRUCTIONS

1. Wash the lemon and peel it. When preparing the marinade, only use half of the liquid at first.
2. Make the marinade: In a small blender, combine the lemon zest, lemon juice, parsley leaves, honey, and 1 tbsp olive oil. Process until a smooth paste forms. Add the salt and pepper to taste.
3. Chicken marinade: Put the chicken in a shallow baking dish and pour the marinade over it. Turn the chicken in the container a couple times to evenly coat it. Refrigerate for several hours or overnight after covering with plastic foil.
4. Marinating for 30 minutes or less may be done on the counter, but if you're marinating for more than that, remove it from the fridge at least 30 minutes before to cooking.
5. Cook: Preheat a cast-iron skillet over high heat. Heat the remaining oil, add the chicken, reduce the heat to

medium-low, and cook for 20 to 25 minutes, flipping the chicken several times but without disturbing it during the first 6-7 minutes.

6. If the chicken breasts become too black too soon after the first 6-7 minutes, reduce the heat and stir the chicken in the skillet.

7. Insert a skewer into the thickest portion of the chicken breast to see whether it is cooked through; the juices should run clear.

8. You can start testing for doneness a few minutes before the first 20 minutes are up, especially if the chicken pieces are under7 ounces.

9. Smaller chicken breast portions, measuring 4.2–5.3 ounces, should take 18–20 minutes to cook.

10. Alternatively, use a meat thermometer to ensure that the interior temperature is between 73 and 82 degrees Celsius/165 and 180 degrees Fahrenheit.

11. Serve immediately with your favorite side dishes (almost anything goes), or chill and serve on a salad.

Prep Time: 5 Mins

Standing Cook: 5 Mins

Total Time: 10 Mins

Servings: 2

INGREDIENTS

- 3 tbsp divided kosher salt
- 1 beef steak (1 pound), 1 inch thick

INSTRUCTIONS

1. To begin, take out the steak from the fridge and season with 2 tbsp salt; set aside for 45-60 minutes.
2. Now preheat a cast-iron skillet over high heat for 4-5 minutes, or until very hot. In the bottom of the skillet, sprinkle the remaining 1 tsp salt; blot the beef dry with paper towels. Then put the steak in the pan and cook for one to two minutes, or until it can be moved easily; turn and place steak in another part of the skillet. Cook for 30 seconds before moving the steak about the pan, pushing gently to maintain even contact.
3. Continue rotating and flipping until cooked to desired doneness (a thermometer should register 135° for medium-rare, 140° for medium, and 145° for medium-well), 1-2 minutes.

Prep Time: 5 Mins

Cook Time: 10 Mins

Additional Time: 30 Mins

Total Time: 45 Mins

Servings: 2

INGREDIENTS

- 2 Filet Mignon (approx 1" thick)
- 3 tbsp Oil
- Pinch Kosher or Sea Salt
- 2 tbsp Unsalted Butter
- Fresh Thyme or Rosemary

INSTRUCTIONS

1. Give the steaks 30 minutes to get to room temperature. Dry well and season generously. Dry well and season liberally.
2. Preheat the oven to 400 degrees Fahrenheit.
3. Warm the oil in a cast-iron pan (or another pan that can go in the oven) for two to three minutes over medium or high heat.
4. Place the Filet Mignon in a heated pan with care (watch out for oil splatter). Now cook for 2-3 minutes, or until a deep brown crust forms on the first side down. The steaks are then flipped and topped with butter and herbs.
5. After turning off the flame, place the pan in the preheated oven.
6. Cook for 2-6 minutes in the oven, or until done to preference.

Prep Time: 5 Mins

Cook Time: 5 Mins

Total Time: 10 Mins

Servings: 4

INGREDIENTS

- 2 tbsp olive oil extra virgin
- 1 pound peeled and deveined shrimp raw
- kosher salt and freshly ground black pepper
- 1 tbsp minced garlic
- 4 tbsp melted grass-fed butter
- 1 tsp Italian seasoning
- 1 lemon juice or more, to taste
- 1 tbsp chopped fresh parsley

INSTRUCTIONS

1. To begin, warm the olive oil in a large pan over medium-high heat. Salt and pepper the shrimp.
2. Cook for 3 minutes or until pink. Remember to stir periodically. Place aside.
3. Cook and toss the garlic a couple times in the skillet for approximately 1 minute. Lemon juice, butter, and Italian spice.
4. Toss in the shrimp and toss lightly to mix. Cook for a further minute.
5. Serve immediately with fresh parsley on top.

Prep Time: 20 Mins

Cook Time: 16 Mins

Total Time: 36 Mins

Servings: 4

INGREDIENTS

- 4 ounces pizza dough (see notes)
- 6 ounces pizza sauce
- 3/4 cup of mozzarella cheese
- 1/4 cup of parmesan cheese
- 2 tbsp oil

TOPPING

- 1 tbsp chopped fresh basil red
- pepper flakes

INSTRUCTIONS

1. Preheat the oven to 500 degrees Fahrenheit. Preheat the oven and place the cast-iron skillet inside. The crispier the pizza, the hotter the pan!
2. Make a 10-inch round out of the dough (unless your skillet measurements are different).
3. Tip: Make sure your pizza shapes and toppings are done before removing the skillet; you don't want your pan to cool down. Take off the hot skillet from the oven with care. To distribute oil in a hot pan, gently use a wad of paper towels/napkins. Place dough circle in pan with care and adjust to suit the edges.

4. Distribute a thin layer of pizza sauce on top, allowing space for the crust to develop (the crust will rise on its own). Top with a liberal quantity of mozzarella and parmesan cheese.

5. Bake for 14-16 minutes, uncovered until cheese is bubbling and caramelized, and the crust is golden brown. When the pizza is done, gently transfer it off the pan onto a cutting board using a fork. If preferred, garnish with fresh basil and red pepper flakes. Extra toppings are included in the notes.

6. To create a second pizza, repeat the baking procedure with more dough or use two pans at once.

NOTES

1. Room temperature dough: Before you form your dough, make sure it's at room temperature. When the dough becomes too cold, it snaps back into form and becomes difficult to deal with. The dough is soft and moldable at room temperature!

2. Cast Iron Pans: You may make this in practically any cast iron pan, such as an original 10-inch cast iron pan, a cast iron Dutch oven (without the top), or a cast iron casserole skillet (without lid).

Prep Time: 15 Mins

Cook Time: 10 Mins

Total Time: 25 Mins

Servings: 3

INGREDIENTS

- 2-3 boneless New York strip steaks, 3/4 to 1 inch thick
- 2 tsp olive oil
- 3 tsp butter
- Salt and pepper to taste
- 1 sprig of fresh rosemary
- 1 bunch of fresh thyme
- 2-3 peeled and smashed garlic cloves

INSTRUCTIONS

1. Start preparing the steaks with salt and pepper on both sides. Allow the steaks to room temperature before cooking.
2. Warm the cast iron skillet over medium-high heat.
3. Toss the steaks in the pan with olive oil.
4. Cook without moving for 3-5 minutes on one side. After that, turn the steak for another 2 minutes. Place the steak on the side to sear the sides.
5. Add the butter, garlic, rosemary, and thyme to the pan once the meat has been seared. Pour the butter over the

meat while it is melting. Cook for another 2 to 3 minutes, or until the desired doneness is achieved.

6. Now take off the steak from the oven and set it aside for 5 minutes to rest before slicing.

HOMEMADE CAST IRON SKILLET STEAK

Prep Time: 5 Mins

Cook Time: 10 Mins

Total Time: 15 Mins

Servings: 2

INGREDIENTS

- 2 steaks, about 1- 1 ½ in thickness
- 1 tbsp avocado oil
- ¼ tsp black pepper
- ½ tsp salt
- 2 tbsp unsalted butter
- 3 sprigs fresh rosemary or thyme
- 2-4 smashed garlic cloves

INSTRUCTIONS

1. Give the steaks 30 minutes to come to room temperature. Then, using a paper towel, blot them dry and season with salt and pepper.
2. Now warm the avocado oil in a cast iron pan over medium-high heat until it shimmers.
3. Put the steaks in the pan and leave them alone for 4 minutes on one side. Cook for another four minutes on the opposite side after flipping the steaks using tongs.
4. Decrease the heat to low and add the butter, garlic, and rosemary or thyme sprigs, stirring constantly. Tilt the

skillet and distribute the butter over the steaks until they are done to your preference, bearing in mind that the temperature will raise another 5° after you take the steaks from the fire.

5. After transferring the steaks to a cutting board or plate, allow them to sit undisturbed for five minutes before slicing or serving. Serve with the melted butter from the skillet, as well as the garlic and rosemary.

NOTES

1. Before seasoning and grilling the steak, allow it to come to room temperature.
2. Before placing the steaks in the pan, let it to heat up.
3. Allow 5 minutes for the steaks to rest before slicing and serving.

Prep Time: 10 Mins

Cook Time: 20 Mins

Total Time: 30 Mins

Servings: 4

INGREDIENTS

- 4 tbsp unsalted butter or ghee
- 2 tbsp oil
- 1/2 head chopped green cabbage
- 1/2 chopped onion
- 1pound washed, and thinly sliced kale
- 2 tbsp low sodium vegetable stock
- 2 tbsp chopped fresh parsley
- 4 minced garlic cloves
- 1/2 tsp salt and pepper, or as desired
- 1/2 tsp red chili pepper flakes, or to taste

INSTRUCTIONS

1. To make the cabbage and kale skillet: Warm the butter and oil in a large pan or skillet over medium high heat. Saute the onion until softened, about 3 minutes.
2. Add the cabbage and simmer for approximately 4-5 minutes, stirring occasionally.
3. Add chopped kale, garlic, salt, pepper, and red chili pepper flakes after the cabbage has softened and begun

to caramelize on the edges. Allow 8-10 minutes for cooking. The vegetables must be well-browned and softened before serving.

4. To deglaze, pour in the vegetable stock and boil for 2 minutes to gently decrease the sauce. To collect the lovely, browned pieces, scrape the bottom of the pan with a wooden spoon.

5. Cook the cabbage and greens for 30 seconds, or until aromatic. Sprinkle with salt, pepper, and parsley to taste before serving the Sauteed Garlic Cabbage Kale Skillet. Enjoy!

Total Time: 25 Mins

Servings: 6

INGREDIENTS

- 2 cups of uncooked corkscrew or spiral pasta
- 3/4-pound fresh asparagus, cut into 1-inch pieces
- 1 medium sweet yellow pepper, julienned
- 1 tbsp olive oil
- 6 medium tomatoes, diced
- 6 ounces boneless fully cooked ham, cubed
- 1/4 cup of minced fresh parsley
- 1/2 tsp salt
- 1/2 tsp dried oregano
- 1/2 tsp dried basil
- 1/4 tsp cayenne pepper
- 1/4 cup of shredded Parmesan cheese

INSTRUCTIONS

1. At first, cook the pasta as directed on the packet. Meanwhile, sauté asparagus and yellow pepper in oil in a large cast-iron or other heavy pan until crisp-tender. Heat through the tomatoes and ham. Drain the noodles and add it to the mixture. Season with parsley and salt and pepper. grate some cheese on top.

Prep Time: 20 Mins

Total Time: 25 Mins

Servings: 4

INGREDIENTS

- 1 cup of long-grain white rice
- 1 tbsp. olive oil
- 1 medium finely chopped onion
- 2 finely chopped garlic cloves
- 1/4 cup of chopped pimiento-stuffed olives
- 1/4 cup of chopped raisins
- 1 tsp. ground cumin
- Kosher salt
- Pepper
- 1 1/4-pound ground beef
- 14-ounce can tomato sauce
- 1/4 tsp. ground cinnamon
- 1 tbsp. red wine vinegar
- Fresh cilantro, for serving

INSTRUCTIONS

1. At first, cook the rice as directed on the packet.
2. Meanwhile, in a large pan over medium-high heat, heat the oil. Cook, covered, for 5 minutes, until the onion is

just soft, stirring periodically. Cook for 1 minute after adding the garlic, then remove from the heat.

3. Preheat the broiler. Place one-half of the onion mixture inside of a large bowl. Mix in the olives, raisins, cumin, and 1/4 tsp each of salt and pepper, then add the meat.

4. Form the mixture into 1-inch balls (approximately 20) and place on a broiler-safe baking sheet coated with foil. Broil for 8 minutes, or until well done.

5. Return the pan with the remaining onion mixture to medium heat while the meatballs are cooking. Simmer for 3 minutes, or until the tomato sauce and cinnamon are cooked through; mix in the vinegar.

6. Now toss the meatballs with the sauce to coat them. If preferred, top with cilantro and serve over rice.

BASIL-BUTTER STEAKS WITH ROASTED POTATOES

Total Time: 30 Mins

Servings: 4

INGREDIENTS

- 15 ounces Parmesan and roasted garlic red potato wedges, frozen
- 1/2 tsp salt
- 4 beef tenderloin steaks, each 1-1/4 inch thick and 6 ounces
- 2 cups of grape tomatoes
- 1/2 tsp pepper
- 5 tbsp butter, divided
- 1 tbsp minced fresh basil

INSTRUCTIONS

1. Bake potato wedges as directed on the box.
2. In the meantime, season the steaks with salt and pepper. Brown steaks in 2 tbsp butter in a 10-inch cast-iron or other ovenproof pan. Toss tomatoes into the skillet. Bake, uncovered, at 425° Fahrenheit for 15-20 minutes, or until meat reaches desired doneness (a thermometer

should register 135° for medium-rare, 140° for medium, and 145° for medium- well).

3. Combine basil and the remaining butter in a small bowl. Serve with potatoes and a dollop of sauce on top of the steaks.

SKILLET CHIPOTLE CHICKEN ENCHILADA BAKE

Prep Time: 15 Mins

Cook Time: 20 Mins

Total Time: 35 Mins

Servings: 6

INGREDIENTS

- 3 boneless skinless chicken breasts
- 14-ounce can of Enchilada Sauce
- 1 small jar of green chiles
- 2 chipotles in adobo chopped
- 3 cups of shredded Monterey Jack cheese
- 6 6-inch corn tortillas
- 1 cup black beans
- 1 cup freshly snipped corn
- Scallions and cilantro to garnish

INSTRUCTIONS

1. Stir the chicken, enchilada sauce, green chiles, and chipotle peppers together in a heavy-bottomed saucepan over medium heat for twenty minutes until the chicken

is cooked through. Remove the chicken from the pan and shred it with two forks. Save the entirety of the sauce.

2. Preheat oven to 375 degrees Fahrenheit.
3. Layer the ingredients in a medium sized skillet, starting with a layer of sauce, then 3 tortillas, 1/2 of the chicken, 1/2 of the black beans, 1/2 of the corn, and 1/2 of the cheese. Repeat with the remaining sauce, tortillas, chicken, black beans, corn, and cheese for the second layer. Now cover and cook for 20 to 30 minutes, until bubbling, cheese has melted, and the top has started to brown.
4. To serve, garnish with scallions and cilantro. As required, cut into wedges.

Prep Time: 20 Mins

Cook Time: 25 Mins

Total Time: 45 Mins

Servings: 4

INGREDIENTS

- 1 tbsp. butter
- 3 tbsp. olive oil
- 1 package sliced cremini mushrooms,
- 8 ounces caps sliced shiitake mushrooms
- 1 large finely chopped shallot
- 8 small chicken thighs
- 1/3 cup of dry white wine
- 1/2 cup of low-sodium chicken broth
- 3 sprigs thyme, plus more for garnish
- 1 tbsp. white miso
- 1/4 cup of heavy cream

INSTRUCTIONS

1. Preheat the oven to 375 degrees Fahrenheit. Then heat butter and 2 tbsp oil in a large oven-safe pan over medium-high heat. Once the butter has foamed, add the mushrooms and a bit
2. of salt, and cook for five minutes, stirring periodically. Add shallot and cook, stirring occasionally, for 2 to 3 minutes, or until mushrooms are golden brown; remove to a platter and wipe skillet clean.
3. Reduce the heat to medium. Season chicken with 1/4 tsp salt and pepper and the remaining 1 tbsp oil. Cook for 10 to 12 minutes, skin side down, in a pan until browned; drain excess grease. Turn the chicken over, then add the wine, broth, and thyme. Now transfer pan to oven and bake for 5 to 6 minutes, or until chicken is cooked through (165°F).
4. Return skillet to medium heat, remove chicken to dish, and discard thyme. Stir in the miso until it has completely dissolved, then cook for 3 minutes. Cook, stirring constantly, until the cream and mushroom mixture are well cooked, about 2 minutes. If preferred, top with chicken and more herbs.

BEEF & PEPPER SKILLET

Total Time: 30 Mins

Servings: 6

INGREDIENTS

- 1-pound lean ground beef (90% lean)
- 1 can undrained diced tomatoes with mild green chilies
- 1 can beef broth
- 1 tbsp chili powder
- 1/4 tsp salt
- 1/8 tsp garlic powder
- 2 cups of instant brown rice
- 1 medium sweet red pepper, sliced
- 1 medium green pepper, sliced
- 1 cup of shredded Colby-Monterey Jack cheese

INSTRUCTIONS

1. Cook beef in a large cast-iron or other heavy pan over medium heat, breaking into crumbles, until no longer pink, 6-8 minutes; drain.

2. Add the tomatoes, broth, chili powder, salt, and garlic powder; bring to a boil. Add the rice and peppers and mix well. Reduce heat to low; cover and cook for 8-10 minutes, or until liquid is absorbed. Remove from the heat and top with cheese. Cover and set aside until the cheese has melted.

CHOCOLATE SKILLET CAKE

Prep Time: 15 Mins

Cook Time: 40 Mins

Total Time: 1 Hr 5 Mins

Servings: 6

INGREDIENTS

- 1 cup of sugar
- ½ cup of brown sugar
- 1 cup of all-purpose flour
- ½ cup of cocoa powder
- 1½ tsp baking powder
- ¾ tsp salt
- ½ cup of half-and-half
- 4 tbsp melted butter
- 1 tsp pure vanilla extract
- 1 cup of hot brewed coffee (see note)
- Confectioners' sugar, for finishing

INSTRUCTIONS

1. Preheat the oven to 350 degrees Fahrenheit. Grease a 9-inch oven-safe pan lightly.
2. Stir together the sugar, brown sugar, flour, cocoa powder, baking powder, and salt in a large bowl. Combine the half-and-half, melted butter, and vanilla essence in a medium mixing bowl.
3. Toss in the half-and-half mixture with the flour and stir just until incorporated. Pour the batter onto the skillet and smooth it out into an equal layer.
4. Pour the coffee over the batter (do not stir!) and let it sit for a few minutes. After that, place the pan in the oven and bake for 25 to 30 minutes, or until the cake has set around the edges but the inside is still a little bit jiggly after it has cooled.
5. Allow 10 minutes for cooling before serving. Serve immediately after garnishing with confectioners' sugar.

NOTES

Although the coffee in this recipe has a mild flavor, you may substitute it with an equal quantity of hot water if you like.

Prep Time: 5 Mins

Cook Time: 15 Mins

Total Time: 20 Mins

Servings: 4

INGREDIENTS

- 2 cups of whole milk
- 1 tbsp. extra virgin olive oil
- 12 ounces spaghetti or thin linguine
- 1 pound asparagus, trimmed and thinly sliced
- 1/4 cup of frozen peas
- 4 ounces soft goat cheese, crumbled
- 3 tbsp. drained capers
- Snipped chives, for garnish

INSTRUCTIONS

1. Mix milk, oil, pasta, 2 1/2 cups water, 1/2 tsp salt, and 1 tsp pepper in a large 12-inch pan. Bring to a boil on high, tossing the pasta with tongs as needed.
2. Add the asparagus and peas. Now reduce heat to low and cook, stirring occasionally, for 10 minutes or until pasta is almost al dente and major of the liquid has been absorbed. Remove the pan from the heat. Add the goat cheese, capers, and 1/4 tsp salt and stir until the cheese is melted. Serve with chives as a garnish.

BAKED CAPRESE CHICKEN SKILLET

Prep Time: 5 Mins

Cook Time: 25 Mins

Total Time: 30 Mins

Servings: 6

INGREDIENTS

- 4 boneless, skinless chicken breasts
- 1 cup of basil pesto
- 1 pint of cherry tomatoes
- 6 ounces. fresh mozzarella cheese, cut into 12 slices
- 3 thickly sliced tomatoes
- 2 tbsp extra-virgin olive oil
- Kosher salt and freshly ground black pepper
- 12 ounces spaghetti
- 2 tbsp balsamic vinegar

- Chopped fresh basil as needed for finishing

INSTRUCTIONS

1. Preheat the oven to 350 degrees Fahrenheit. Grease an oven-safe pan liberally with nonstick cooking spray.
2. Place the chicken breasts in the skillet that has been prepared. Then spread 1 tbsp of pesto on each piece of chicken and then massage it all over to coat it evenly.
3. Top each chicken breast with three mozzarella slices and a few tomato slices. Arrange the cherry tomatoes in a circle around the chicken in the pan—season with salt and pepper and drizzle with olive oil.
4. After that, put the baking dish in the oven and bake for 20 to 22 minutes, or until the cheese is melted, the tomatoes are soft, and the chicken is well cooked.
5. Boil a big saucepan of salted water while the chicken cooks. Cook until the pasta is al dente (or according to the package instructions). Toss the pasta with the leftover pesto after draining it.
6. To serve, divide the spaghetti among four dishes and top with a piece of chicken for each serving. Drizzle 1/2 tbsp balsamic vinegar over each plate and top with fresh basil.

SKILLET LEMON CHICKEN WITH ARTICHOKES

Total Time: 30 Mins

Servings: 4

INGREDIENTS

- 1 1/2 cups of white or brown rice
- 6 small chicken thighs, about 2 pounds
- 14-ounce artichoke hearts
- 1 medium onion
- 1 lemon
- 1/2 bunch parsley
- 2/3 cup of dry white wine
- 1 tbsp butter

INSTRUCTIONS

1. Preheat the oven to 425 degrees Fahrenheit. Wrap foil around a large rimmed baking sheet.

2. Follow the package directions to cook 1 1/2 cups white or brown rice. Begin cooking the chicken while the rice is cooking.

3. Warm 1 tsp of vegetable oil in a 12-inch skillet over medium heat. Season six small chicken thighs with half a tsp each of salt and black pepper. Now place the chicken skin side down in the skillet. Cook for 5 to 8 minutes, or until golden brown. Remove the pan from the heat. Prepare your veggies while the chicken cooks.

4. Rinse and quarter 1 14-ounce can artichoke hearts. Chop one medium onion very finely. Remove the seeds and thinly slice 1 lemon. Chop half of a bunch of parsley. Set aside.

5. After that, place the chicken on the foil-lined baking sheet, skin side up. Place the chicken in the oven and bake for 12 to 15 minutes, or until cooked through. Meanwhile, get the sauce going.

6. Now return the skillet to medium heat and then add the chopped onion. Then season with 1/4 tsp salt and simmer for 3 minutes, stirring periodically.

7. Bring 2/3 cup dry white wine to a low simmer. Simmer for 2 minutes, scraping up any brown pieces from the bottom of the pan.

8. At this point, melt 1 tbsp of butter in the same skillet. Add the artichoke hearts and lemon slices when the butter has melted.

9. Sprinkle the chopped parsley over the chicken and spoon the sauce over it. Serve with rice that has been prepared.

SAUSAGE HASH

Prep Time: 10 Mins

Cook Time: 30 Mins

Total Time: 40 Mins

Servings: 6

INGREDIENTS

- 1 pound bulk pork sausage
- 1 medium onion, chopped
- 2 medium carrots, grated
- 1 medium chopped green pepper
- 3 cups of diced cooked potatoes
- 1/2 tsp salt
- 1/4 tsp pepper

INSTRUCTIONS

1. Cook the sausage in a large cast-iron or other heavy pan over medium heat until no longer pink; drain. Cook until the onion, carrots, and green pepper are soft. Now combine the potatoes, salt, and pepper in a mixing bowl. Then reduce heat to low; simmer and stir for 20 minutes, or until lightly browned and cooked through.

Total Time: 30 Mins

Servings: 4

INGREDIENTS

- 2 tbsp butter
- 1 pound chicken breasts, boneless and cut into strips
- 1 medium chopped onion
- 1 large thinly sliced carrot
- 2 minced garlic cloves
- 1 tbsp cornstarch
- 1 can chicken broth
- 2 tbsp lemon juice
- 1/4 tsp salt

- 1 cup of frozen peas
- 1-1/2 cups of uncooked instant rice

INSTRUCTIONS

1. Cook the chicken, onion, carrot, and garlic in butter in a large cast-iron or other heavy pan over medium-high heat until the chicken is no longer pink, approximately 5-7 minutes.
2. Mix cornstarch, broth, lemon juice, and salt in a small bowl until smooth. Gradually pour the liquid into the skillet and bring to a boil. Cook and whisk for 1-2 minutes, or until the sauce has thickened.
3. Now return to a boil after adding the peas. Add the rice and mix well. Remove from heat and let aside for 5 minutes, covered.

LEMON CHICKEN AND RICE SKILLET

Prep Time: 10 Mins

Cook Time: 40 Mins

Total Time: 50 Mins

Servings: 4

INGREDIENTS

- 1 tbsp extra-virgin olive oil
- 3 garlic cloves, minced
- 1 onion, diced
- 1-pound boneless chicken breast, diced into 1–1/2 pieces

- 2 cups of chicken broth
- 1 cup of uncooked long-grain white rice
- 1/4 cup of fresh parsley, minced
- 2 tbsp lemon juice
- 1–1/2 tsp fine sea salt
- 1/2 tsp garlic powder
- 1/4 tsp ground black pepper
- Pinch red pepper flakes (optional)
- Sliced lemon, optional

INSTRUCTIONS

1. First, warm the oil in a large skillet over medium heat. Cook, often stirring, until the garlic and onions begin to soften, approximately 2-3 minutes.
2. Now cook until the chicken is no longer pink on the exterior, about 3-5 minutes.
3. Stir together the chicken broth, rice, parsley, lemon juice, salt, garlic powder, black pepper, and pepper flakes.
4. Then bring them to boil, then turn down to the lowest setting on the stove. Add the sliced lemon to the rice, cover, and cook for 30 minutes, or until the rice is fluffy and there is no more liquid.
5. Add more pepper, red pepper flakes, and parsley to taste.

NOTES

Do you want to make this with cooked rice or cauliflower rice? You might try skipping the liquid and simply sauteing the rice till it's warmed through. It would essentially transform into a stir-fry!

Prep Time: 15 Mins

Cook Time: 45 Mins

Total Time: 1 Hr

Servings: 8

INGREDIENTS

- 1 cup of all-purpose flour
- 2/3 cup of old-fashioned oats
- 1/2 cup of light brown sugar
- 1/2 cup of chopped walnuts

- 1/4 tsp. plus pinch salt
- 6 tbsp. plus 4 tbsp. butter, divided, cut up and cold
- 1/2 tsp. ground cinnamon
- 1/4 tsp. ground allspice
- 2 pounds peeled, cored and chopped ripe pears
- 1/2 cup of granulated sugar
- 2 cups of frozen mixed berries
- 3 tbsp. cornstarch
- 1/4 cup of amaretto or almond liqueur

INSTRUCTIONS

1. Preheat the oven to 375 degrees Fahrenheit. Combine flour, oats, brown sugar, walnuts, and 1/4 tsp salt in a medium bowl. Rub 6 tbsp butter into the mixture with your fingertips; squeeze to make big clumps. Put it in the freezer.

2. Now heat the remaining 4 tbsp butter in an oven-safe 10-inch pan on medium for 6 minutes, or until browned and aromatic, stirring often. Cook, stirring constantly, for 1 minute after adding the cinnamon and spices. Cook for 5 minutes, stirring often, with the pears, granulated sugar, and a touch of salt. Remove the pan from the heat. Combine the berries, cornstarch, and amaretto in a mixing bowl. Crumb topping should be sprinkled over the pear mixture. Bake for 25 minutes, or until the pears are soft and the topping has browned. Warm or at room temperature is OK.

SKILLET CHICKEN WITH CREAMY SPRING VEGETABLE

Prep Time: 15 Mins

Cook Time: 40 Mins

Total Time: 55 Mins

Servings: 6

INGREDIENTS

- 6 bone-in, skin-on chicken thighs

- Kosher salt and freshly ground pepper
- 2 tbsp unsalted butter
- 1 1/2 cups of low sodium chicken broth
- 1/4 cup of heavy cream
- 1 1/2 tbsp all-purpose flour
- 3 minced garlic cloves
- 1 minced shallot
- 3 carrots, peeled and cut into 1/3-inch diagonal slices
- 8 ounces cremini mushrooms
- 1/4 cup of dry white wine (see notes)
- 1-pound trimmed asparagus
- 1 1/2 tbsp chopped fresh dill
- 1 tbsp chopped fresh tarragon

INSTRUCTIONS

1. Preheat the oven to 400 degrees Fahrenheit.
2. Then season chicken thighs to taste with salt and pepper.
3. In a large oven-safe skillet, melt butter over medium-high heat. Sear both sides of the chicken, skin-side down, until golden brown, about 2- 3 minutes each side.
4. After that, place in the oven and roast for 25-30 minutes, or until thoroughly cooked through and the internal temperature reaches 175 degrees Fahrenheit. Keep the chicken warm by setting it aside.
5. Stir together chicken broth, heavy cream, and flour in a medium bowl; put aside.
6. Now add garlic and shallot to the pan and heat, stirring constantly, for approximately two minutes, until fragrant. Cook, stirring occasionally, until the carrots and mushrooms are barely cooked, about 4-5 minutes.
7. Bring the wine and stock combination to a simmer, scraping any browned pieces from the bottom of the skillet.

8. Stir in the asparagus and cook for 3-4 minutes, or until crisp tender. Stir in the dill and tarragon for 1 minute, or until fragrant; season with salt and pepper to taste. Return the chicken to the pan.

9. Serve right away.

NOTES

As a non-alcoholic substitute for white wine, more chicken broth may be used.

CAJUN SHRIMP SKILLET

Total Time: 25 Mins

Servings: 4

INGREDIENTS

- 3 tbsp butter
- 2 minced garlic cloves
- 1/2 cup of amber beer or beef broth
- 1 tsp Worcestershire sauce

- 1 tsp pepper
- 1/2 tsp salt
- 1/2 tsp dried thyme
- 1/2 tsp crushed dried rosemary
- 1/2 tsp crushed red pepper flakes
- 1/4 tsp cayenne pepper
- 1/8 tsp dried oregano
- 1 pound large peeled and deveined uncooked shrimp
- Hot cooked grits (optional)

INSTRUCTIONS

1. Melt butter in a big cast-iron or other heavy pan over medium-high heat. Cook for 1 minute, stirring constantly. Bring to a boil with the beer, Worcestershire sauce, and spices. Cook, stirring periodically, for 3-4 minutes, or until shrimp become pink. Serve over grits if desired.

PORK CHOPS WITH ROSEMARY TRUFFLE SAUCE

Prep Time: 15 Mins

Cook Time: 15 Mins

Total Time: 30 Mins

Servings: 4

INGREDIENTS

- 2 tbsp. extra virgin olive oil
- 4 bone-in pork chops (each about 1" thick)
- 3 medium chopped shallots
- 12 ounces thinly sliced cremini mushrooms
- 1/2 tsp. chopped fresh rosemary
- 2/3 cup of half-and-half
- 2 tbsp. truffle butter

INSTRUCTIONS

1. Add the oil and heat in a 12-inch skillet over medium-high heat until it is hot but not smoking. Season pork chops with 1/2 tsp salt and pepper all over. Cook pork chops for 6 minutes, turning once, until browned on both sides; transfer to a large dish. Reduce the heat to medium-low and drain the excess fat from the skillet. Add shallots, mushrooms, rosemary, and 1/8 tsp salt to the skillet. Cook for 5 minutes, stirring occasionally.
2. Combine the half-and-half and butter in a bowl. Place the meat in the sauce and cover it. Then cook for 4 to 6 minutes, or until meat is fully cooked (145°F).

CREAMY PARMESAN PESTO CHICKEN SKILLET

Total Time: 30 Mins

Prep Time: 15 Mins

Cook Time: 15 Mins

Servings: 4

INGREDIENTS

- 2 large boneless skinless chicken breasts, horizontally cut
- Olive oil for cooking
- Pesto chicken rub
- 3 tbsp pesto
- 1 tbsp olive oil
- 2 tbsp finely grated Parmesan cheese
- 1 tbsp Dijon mustard
- 1 tsp honey
- 1/2 tsp salt
- 1/4 tsp pepper

Parmesan pesto sauce

- 1 tbsp olive oil
- 1 tbsp butter
- 8 ounces thinly sliced cremini mushrooms
- 1 chopped shallot
- 1/2 tsp dried oregano
- 1/4 tsp dried thyme
- 1/4 tsp red pepper flakes
- 1 tbsp flour
- 6 minced garlic cloves
- 2 cups of low sodium chicken broth, divided
- 1 tbsp cornstarch
- 1/4 cup of heavy cream or half-and-half (or more to taste)
- 1/4 cup of pesto
- 1 tsp chicken bouillon (optional)
- 1 pound asparagus, ends trimmed, cut into 1" pieces
- 1 cup of thawed frozen petite peas
- 1/3 cup of freshly grated Parmesan

1. Chicken: Stir together all of the ingredients for the Pesto Chicken Rub in a small bowl. Allow the chicken to remain at room temperature for up to 30 minutes while you prepare your vegetables, or refrigerate for up to 8 hours before cooking.

2. Add 1 tbsp oil in a big pan and heat over medium-high heat. Add the chicken to the pan when it is quite hot and cook for 2-3 minutes, or until browned. Flip the chicken, cover, and decrease the heat to medium. Cook for another 4-7 minutes, or until chicken is cooked through (depending on thickness). Transfer to a plate and keep heated with foil.

3. Sauce: Reduce the heat to medium and add 1 tbsp butter and 1 tbsp olive oil to the pan (do not wipe out skillet). Cook for 4 minutes, stirring frequently, then add shallots, oregano, thyme, and red pepper flakes; cook for another 3 minutes, stirring frequently. Cook for 1 minute, often stirring, after adding the flour and garlic (it will be thick).

4. Reduce the heat to a minimum. Stir in half of the chicken broth slowly. Half of the remaining stock, along with 1 tbsp of cornstarch, is whisked together and gradually added to the skillet, followed by the cream/half and half. Bring to a low simmer for 1 minute or until the sauce has thickened somewhat. Simmer for two minutes until asparagus is crisp and tender and the sauce has thickened, adding 1/4 cup pesto, chicken bouillon (optional) and asparagus. Dilute the sauce with chicken broth or cream if it becomes too thick.

5. Stir in the peas and Parmesan until the cheese has melted. Return the chicken to the skillet. Sprinkle with salt and pepper to taste. Now garnish with freshly grated Parmesan cheese and serve with/over noodles, potatoes, or rice.

NOTES

If you want to conserve calories, you can leave off the half and half/heavy cream, but if you want to add some additional richness, it's delicious.

UPSIDE-DOWN MEAT PIE

Prep Time: 25 Mins

Bake Time: 20 Mins

Total Time: 45 Mins

Servings: 4

INGREDIENTS

- 1 pound of ground beef
- 1/2 cup of chopped onion
- 1/2 tsp salt
- 15 ounces tomato sauce

Baking Powder Biscuits:

- 1 cup of all-purpose flour
- 2 tsp baking powder
- 1 tsp celery salt
- 1 tsp paprika
- 1/2 tsp salt
- 1/4 tsp pepper
- 3 tbsp butter
- 1/2 cup of 2% milk

INSTRUCTIONS

1. First, cook ground beef and onion in a large cast-iron or other ovenproof pan until beef is browned and onion is soft; crumble meat; drain. Simmer for 10-15 minutes after adding salt and tomato sauce.
2. Meanwhile, whisk the flour, baking powder, celery salt, paprika, salt, and pepper in a bowl. Now cut in the butter with a pastry cutter until the mixture resembles coarse meal. Stir in the milk until a soft dough forms. Using a tbsp, drop it into the meat mixture.
3. Bake, uncovered, at 475° for 20 minutes, or until brown.

Prep Time: 35 Mins

Total Time: 1 Hr 25 Mins

Servings: 12

INGREDIENTS

- 2 recipes Ultimate Pie Dough, not divided or chilled
- 1/4 cup of butter
- 4 pounds peeled, cored and chopped Golden Delicious apples
- 2/3 cup of packed brown sugar
- 1/3 cup of granulated sugar
- 1/2 tsp. ground cinnamon
- 1/2 tsp. ground ginger
- 1/8 tsp. ground allspice
- 1/4 cup of cornstarch
- 3 tbsp. lemon juice
- 2 tbsp. heavy cream
- 1/4 cup of coarse sugar

INSTRUCTIONS

1. Make 12 mounds of Ultimate Pie Dough. Wrap each with plastic wrap. Roll each one to a 6" round one at a time. Refrigerate dough before fitting into 3.5" cast-iron skillets (or divide dough into 6 mounds and shape into 8" rounds for six 5" cast-iron skillets). Repeat with the remaining dough and skillets.

2. Preheat the oven to 375 degrees Fahrenheit. Then melt butter in a 12- inch skillet over medium-high heat. Combine the apples, brown and granulated sugars, cinnamon, ginger, and allspice. Cook for 5 minutes, stirring occasionally. Take off the pan from the heat and stir in the cornstarch and lemon juice. Toss to evenly coat. Fill tiny skillets halfway with the filling. Fold the dough's edges up and over the filling. Brush cream over the edges and sprinkle coarse sugar on top. Place two cookie sheets on top of each other to hold the skillets. Bake for 1 hour to 1 hour 10 minutes, or until golden

brown around the edges. Allow to cool on a wire rack. Baked and chilled for up to 1 day, uncovered.

Prep Time: 10 Mins

Cook Time: 35 Mins

Total Time: 45 Mins

Servings: 8

INGREDIENTS

- 2 tbsp olive oil
- 1 diced onion
- 2 minced garlic cloves
- ⅓ cup of chopped pickled jalapeños
- 1 pound of ground beef
- 2½ tbsp taco seasoning
- Salt and freshly ground black pepper
- 1 cup of salsa
- One 14-ounce can dice fire-roasted tomatoes
- 1½ cups of shredded Monterey Jack cheese
- 1½ cups of shredded cheddar cheese
- ¼ cup of sliced green onions Tortilla chips, for serving

INSTRUCTIONS

1. Preheat the oven to 400 degrees Fahrenheit. A large cast-iron (or other oven-safe) sauté pan is heated over medium heat with olive oil.
2. Whenever the oil is heated, add the onion and cook for 4 to 5 minutes, or until tender. Now cook for another 1 minute, or until the garlic and jalapenos are aromatic.
3. Cook for 6 to 7 minutes, or until the ground beef is nicely browned. After adding the taco spice, season with salt and pepper. Bring the salsa and tomatoes to a low simmer. Cook for two to three minutes, occasionally stirring.
4. Remove the skillet from the heat and evenly distribute both slices of cheese. Bake them for 8-10 minutes, or until the cheese has melted and the chili is bubbling.

5. Leave for 5 to 10 minutes cooling before serving heated with green onions. Serve with tortilla chips on the side.

Total Time: 30 Mins

Servings: 4

INGREDIENTS

- 4 chicken breast halves, boneless and skinless (5 ounces each)
- 1/4 cup of 2% milk
- 1/2 tsp minced garlic
- 1/4 cup of all-purpose flour
- 1 tbsp ranch salad dressing mix
- 1/8 tsp pepper
- 1 tbsp olive oil
- 1 tbsp butter

INSTRUCTIONS

1. Set aside after gently flattening the chicken. Combine milk and garlic in a small bowl. Stir to combine, salad dressing mix, and pepper in a separate shallow bowl. Now dip the chicken in the milk mixture, then in the flour mixture.
2. Cook chicken in oil and butter in a large cast-iron or other heavy pan over medium heat until no longer pink, 6-8 minutes.

Total Time: 20 Mins

Servings: 4

INGREDIENTS

- 1 tsp. extra-virgin olive oil
- 3 slices chopped thick-cut bacon (freeze briefly or snip with shears for ease in cutting)
- 1 medium thinly sliced shallot 6 large eggs
- 1/4 cup of milk
- 1/8 tsp.
- Kosher salt
- 1/8 tsp. Freshly ground black pepper
- 1 cup of shredded Gruyère cheese
- Chives, for garnish
- Green salad, for serving

INSTRUCTIONS

1. Heat olive oil in an 8" oven-safe nonstick pan on medium. Cook for 6 minutes, stirring periodically, after adding the bacon and shallot.
2. Now combine the eggs, milk, salt, and pepper in a bowl; toss in the Gruyère. Crack eggs into a skillet. Cook for 3 minutes, stirring regularly to produce curds and enable the runny egg to seep to the pan's bottom.
3. Then bake for 8 minutes at 375 degrees Fahrenheit until the top is set. Serve with chives as a garnish. Serve with a salad of greens.

Total Time: 30 Mins

Servings: 6

INGREDIENTS

- 1 tbsp butter
- 1/3 cup of chopped onion
- 1/4 cup of all-purpose flour
- 1 can condensed chicken broth, undiluted
- 1/4 cup of fat-free milk
- 1/8 tsp pepper
- 2 cups of cubed cooked turkey breast
- 2 cups of frozen peas and carrots, thawed
- 12 ounces refrigerated buttermilk biscuits, quartered

INSTRUCTIONS

1. Preheat the oven to 400 degrees Fahrenheit. Then melt butter over medium-high heat in a 10-inch cast-iron or another ovenproof pan. Cook, often stirring, until the onion is soft, about 2-3 minutes.

2. Now mix flour, broth, milk, and pepper in a small bowl until combined; add into the pan. Bring to a boil, stirring frequently; simmer and stir for 1-2 minutes, or until thickened. Heat through the turkey and frozen veggies. Place biscuits on top of the stew. Finally, bake them for 15-20 minutes, or until golden brown.

Total Time: 1 Hr 20 Mins

Servings: 12

INGREDIENTS

For the Sauce

- 2 tbsp oil
- 1 roughly chopped yellow onion
- 3 tsp chili powder
- 2 tsp cumin
- 1 tsp oregano
- 1 1/2 tsp salt
- 4 roughly chopped garlic cloves
- 1 1/2 cups of chicken broth
- 28-ounce diced tomatoes

For the Chicken Tortilla Pie

- 2 pounds boneless skinless chicken breasts
- 2 tbsp southwestern or taco seasoning
- 30 mall corn tortillas
- 3 cups of shredded Mozzarella cheese
- Cilantro and Cotija cheese for topping

INSTRUCTIONS

1. Sauce: Add the oil and heat in a big skillet. Cook for 5-10 minutes after adding the onions. Then decrease the heat to low and add the garlic, chili powder, cumin, oregano, salt, and chili powder. Frying garlic for two to three minutes, or until very fragrant, taking care not to burn it. Add the chicken stock, garlic, and tomatoes as required and simmer for 5-10 minutes until the sauce is very dark

red. Blend half of the sauce (there is a lot of spice) in a blender. As required, taste and adjust the saltiness.

2. Chicken: Add spice to the chicken breasts. Add the chicken to the pan from step one that has been heated over medium low heat with a little oil—Cook for a few minutes on each side, or until golden brown. Cover with sauce and continue to boil for 5-10 minutes to allow the chicken to finish cooking in the sauce gradually. Remove the chicken from the sauce with two forks and shred it. Set aside some time.

3. Assemble: Set the oven temperature to 375° Fahrenheit. Dip five tortillas in the heated sauce and arrange them in a 9-inch circular pan or baking dish. Combine a scoop of chicken, a handful of cheese, and roughly 3/4 cup of sauce in a bowl. Repeat the layering process. Finish with a final layer of tortillas, a scoop of sauce, and a sprinkling of cheese. (Now go make some more!)

4. Bake: Cover the cheese with foil that has been coated with a nonstick oil to keep it from sticking. Now bake them for 20 to 30 minutes, or until the cheese is Ooey-Gooey-Perfection and the sauce is bubbling. Garnish with cilantro and Cotija cheese.

NOTES

1. This is a gentle recipe. I would add a couple of chipotle peppers or jalapenos to the sauce if you wanted to take it up a level.

2. You may substitute bottled enchilada sauce for the sauce if you are in a hurry. But I'll tell you: I tried it that way, and it's not near as tasty as the handmade version.

Total Time: 20 Mins

Servings: 4

INGREDIENTS

- 4 ounces Pepper Jack cheese
- 1 cup of quinoa
- 8 ounces broccoli florets
- 4 cup of baby spinach
- 1/2 cup of light sour cream
- 3 garlic cloves

INSTRUCTIONS

1. Shred four ounces of Pepper Jack. Set aside.
2. Bring one cup of quinoa and four cups of water to a boil in a covered saucepot with a capacity of five quarts. Cook as directed on the package, then add 8 ounces broccoli florets 5 minutes before draining the quinoa.
3. Drain the quinoa mixture well. Then combine 4 cups baby spinach, 1/2 cup light sour cream, 1/2 tsp salt, 3 garlic cloves, and 1/2 tsp pepper.
4. Spread the mixture in a 10-inch oven-safe pan. Add the shredded cheese on top. Now broil for three minutes on high, or until melted.

Total Time: 30 Mins

Servings: 6

INGREDIENTS

- 6 boneless skinless chicken thighs
- 1/2 tsp salt
- 1/4 tsp pepper
- 1 tbsp olive oil
- 10 peeled and halved garlic cloves
- 2 tbsp brandy or chicken stock
- 1 cup of chicken stock
- 1 tsp minced fresh rosemary
- 1/2 tsp chopped fresh thyme
- 1 tbsp chopped fresh chives

INSTRUCTIONS

1. Add salt and pepper to the chicken. Add the oil and heat in a big cast- iron pan or another heavy skillet over medium-high heat. The chicken should be cooked on all sides. Remove the pan from the heat.
2. Remove the skillet from the heat and add the garlic cloves, halved, and brandy. Return to the fire and cook, constantly stirring, until the liquid has almost completely evaporated, about 1-2 minutes.
3. Come back the chicken to the pan after adding the liquid, rosemary, and thyme. Bring the water to a boil. Now reduce heat to low and cook uncovered for 6-8 minutes, or until a thermometer reads 170°. Garnish with chives.

BAKED ONE POT MAC AND CHEESE

Prep Time: 5 Mins

Cook Time: 20 Mins

Total Time: 25 Mins

Servings: 6

INGREDIENTS

- 4 tbsp unsalted butter
- 6 tbsp flour
- 1 tsp salt (See note 1)
- 3 cups milk
- Black pepper
- 2 cups water
- 1/2-pound dried macaroni (elbow pasta) (see note 2)
- 2 cups of grated tasty or cheddar cheese
- 1 cup of grated provolone dolce cheese (See note 3)

Topping

- 1/4 cup of panko breadcrumbs
- 1/4 cup of grated parmesan cheese
- 1/2 tbsp finely chopped fresh parsley(optional)

INSTRUCTIONS

1. Preheat the oven to 180 degrees Celsius/350 degrees Fahrenheit.
2. In a deep fry pan or skillet (See note 4) over medium heat, melt the butter. (See note 5)
3. (See note 5) Cook for 1 minute, stirring regularly.

4. Now, add half of the milk and whisk it in to dissolve the roux. It will thicken rapidly, so add the rest of the milk after that. To dissolve all of the roux into the milk, whisk in tiny circles while turning the pan.

5. Turn the heat to medium high and add the water, salt, and 5 grinds of pepper. Stir slowly so the bottom of the pan does not stick. Add the macaroni when the white sauce begins to steam and thickens to the point where it coats the pan's edges (about 2 to 3 minutes).

6. Reduce the heat to medium and whisk gently with a wooden spoon to thoroughly combine the macaroni and ensure it does not cling to the bottom. Cook for one minute. Make sure not to cook it any longer after adding the macaroni, since this will affect the dish's "sauciness" and ensure the macaroni isn't overdone.

7. Cover the fry pan with foil (See note 6), then place it on the middle shelf of the oven.

8. Remove from the oven after 12 minutes of baking. It will appear that there is too much sauce at first, but it will diminish and thicken in the next phases. The pasta should just be slightly al dente (al dente). The leftover heat will continue to cook it.

9. Turn off the oven and preheat the grill/broiler to high.

10. After that, stir in the cheese until it is evenly distributed throughout the macaroni. As you mix, the cheese will melt and the sauce will thicken. Don't stir too much, or the sauce will thicken too much due to evaporation.

11. Place the panko and parmesan cheese on top, then brown in the grill or broiler for a few minutes.

12. Before serving, remove it from the grill/broiler and let it aside for 5 minutes to rest.

NOTES

1. You may need to tweak the quantity of salt if you vary the cheese you use. If you use gruyere instead of

cheddar or delicious cheese, for example, you may need to add a little of salt because gruyere is less salty. Because provolone is saltier, you'll probably need to add a sprinkle of salt if you use mozzarella instead of provolone.

2. This dish is quite sensitive to the type of pasta used. It will work with any pasta that takes 9 to 10 minutes to cook in boiling water, such as macaroni, spirals, tiny shells, and so on (per packet instructions). It won't work with noodles like penne, which take roughly 13 minutes to cook in boiling water since it absorbs more water and takes much longer to cook than this recipe calls for, resulting in a much less saucy Mac & Cheese.

3. Because rigatoni and spaghetti cook too rapidly, you'll finish up with an excessive amount of sauce. If you want to make this with different pastas, play about with the water and roux amounts.

4. Make sure you get Provolone Dolce rather than Provolone Piccante. Dolce is the softest of the bunch; when you squeeze it, it feels like a rubber ball, and it melts like mozzarella cheese. Piccante is a tougher, sharper cheese that resembles parmesan cheese.

5. The fry pan I used has a diameter of 10" and a depth of 2.4". It was Exactly the right size for this recipe. Because this sauce does not spray or bubble, spillage was not a concern during cooking, but I had to be cautious when stirring.

6. A somewhat deeper skillet / fry pan or a big casserole pot works best.

7. If you're using a stove with a thick foundation or a powerful gas burner, reduce the heat to medium low to prevent the butter and roux from browning. Brown sauce isn't supposed to be in macaroni and cheese.

Prep Time: 20 Mins

Cook Time: 15 Mins

Total Time: 35 Mins

Servings: 4

INGREDIENTS

- 2 tbsp. olive oil
- 1 medium sliced zucchini
- 1 medium seeded and chopped red pepper
- 1 medium chopped onion
- 3 chopped garlic cloves
- One 28 ounce can crushed tomatoes
- 6 ounces no-cook lasagna noodles, cut into thirds
- 1 cup of part-skim ricotta cheese
- 1 cup of part-skim mozzarella cheese, shredded
- Fresh basil leaves, for garnish

INSTRUCTIONS

1. Add the oil and heat in a large 12-inch skillet over medium-high heat. Combine zucchini, red pepper, onion, garlic, and 1/2 tsp salt. Cook for 6 minutes, stirring occasionally. Reduce the heat to a low setting. Toss in the tomatoes.

2. Now pour the sauce over the noodles, making sure that each piece is at least half soaked. Then cover and simmer on low for fifteen minutes, or until the noodles are almost al dente, turning gently twice.

3. Then place a dollop of ricotta on top of the noodles, then top with mozzarella. Cook for 10 minutes, or until the cheese has melted and the noodles are al dente. Finally, add a quarter tsp of black pepper and a sprig of basil on top.

Total Time: 20 Mins

Servings: 6

INGREDIENTS

- 2 tbsp minced fresh sage
- 1 tsp garlic powder
- 1 tsp kosher salt
- 1 tsp freshly ground pepper
- 1-1/2 pounds skin-on salmon fillet
- 2 tbsp olive oil

INSTRUCTIONS

1. Preheat the oven to 375 degrees Fahrenheit. Rub the first four ingredients onto the flesh side of the fish. Cut into 6 equal pieces.
2. Add the oil and heat in a big cast-iron pan over medium heat. Cook for 5 minutes with the salmon skin side down. Now place pan in oven and bake for 10 minutes, or until fish flakes easily with a fork.

MONTEREY CHICKEN

Prep Time: 10 Mins

Cook Time: 20 Mins

Total Time: 30 Mins

Servings: 4

INGREDIENTS

- 4 boneless skinless chicken breasts
- 1 tbsp olive oil
- Salt and pepper to taste
- 1 cup of barbecue sauce
- 1 cup of shredded cheese
- 4 slices bacon cooked and crumbled
- 1/2 cup of diced tomatoes
- 1/4 cup of green onions

INSTRUCTIONS

1. At first, warm the olive oil in a large oven-safe skillet over medium heat. Preheat oven to 400 degrees Fahrenheit.
2. After that, sprinkle salt and pepper on both sides of the chicken.
3. Cook for 4-5 minutes on each side, or until the chicken is cooked through. Cooking time varies on chicken thickness.
4. Over the chicken, pour the barbecue sauce. Using a fork, smear 1/4 cup of cheese over each chicken breast.

5. Place the skillet in the oven for 3-5 minutes, or until the cheese is melted.
6. Serve the chicken with bacon, tomatoes, and green onions on top.

Total Time: 40 Mins

Servings: 6

INGREDIENTS

- 12 large eggs
- 1/2 cup of whole milk
- 2 ounces grated Pecorino cheese
- Kosher salt
- Pepper
- 2 tbsp. olive oil
- 1 small finely chopped onion
- 1/2-pound Italian sausage, casings removed
- 1/2 large bunch kale, stems discarded, and leaves chopped
- 1 cup of marinara sauce
- 6 ounces sliced fresh mozzarella
- Fresh basil leaves, for topping

INSTRUCTIONS

1. Preheat the oven to 350 degrees Fahrenheit.
2. Stir together eggs, milk, pecorino, 1/4 tsp salt, and 1/2 tsp pepper in a large bowl.
3. Add oil and heat the oil in a big oven-safe skillet (ideally cast-iron) over medium heat. Add onions and simmer,

covered, while stirring regularly for 5 minutes, until tender. Cook for around 5 minutes, breaking up the sausage with a spoon, until it is browned. Add kale and simmer, turning periodically, for about a minute, or until wilted.

4. Now reduce the heat to low and toss in the egg mixture to evenly distribute the sausage and veggies. Come back to the oven and bake for 18-20 minutes, or until the center is almost set. Take off the pan from the oven and preheat the broiler.

5. Spread the sauce evenly over the frittata, then top with mozzarella. Finally, broil for five minutes, or until the cheese is browned and bubbling. Serve immediately with basil on top.

Total Time: 20 Mins

Servings: 4

INGREDIENTS

- 8 ounces uncooked thick rice noodles
- 1/4 cup of reduced-sodium soy sauce
- 2 tbsp cornstarch
- 3 minced garlic cloves
- 1-pound cubed boneless skinless chicken breasts
- 1 tbsp peanut oil
- 1 tbsp sesame oil
- 6 green onions, cut into 2-inch pieces
- 1 cup of unsalted cashews
- 2 tbsp sweet chili sauce
- Toasted sesame seeds, optional

INSTRUCTIONS

1. First, cook rice noodles as directed on the packet.
2. Meanwhile, stir the soy sauce, cornstarch, and garlic in a small bowl. Toss in the chicken. Sauté the chicken combination in peanut and sesame oils in a large cast-iron or another heavy pan until no longer pink—Cook for a further minute after adding the onions.

3. Now rinse the pasta and add it to the pan. Heat through the cashews and chili sauce. If desired, roasted sesame seeds can be sprinkled on top.

SKILLET CORNBREAD WITH CHEDDAR AND SCALLIONS

Prep Time: 15 Mins

Cook Time: 40 Mins

Total Time: 55 Mins

Servings: 8

INGREDIENTS

- 1 cup of all-purpose flour
- 1 cup of stone-ground yellow cornmeal
- 3 tbsp sugar
- 2 tsp kosher salt
- 2 tsp baking powder
- 1¼ cups of buttermilk
- 2 large eggs
- 7 tbsp unsalted butter, melted and chilled
- ¾ cup of coarsely grated sharp white cheddar cheese
- 6 trimmed and thinly sliced scallions

INSTRUCTIONS

1. Preheat the oven to 425 degrees Fahrenheit. Then place an 8-inch cast- iron pan in the oven at the same time to make it extremely hot.
2. Combine the flour, cornmeal, sugar, baking powder, and salt in a large bowl. Stir the eggs, buttermilk, and 6 tbsp melted butter in a medium bowl until thoroughly combined. Ladle the egg mixture into the flour mixture and thoroughly combine. Add the cheese and scallions and mix well.
3. Wear an oven mitt and gently remove the pan from the oven; stir in the remaining 1 tbsp butter. Tilt the skillet to evenly distribute the butter on the bottom and sides. Scrape the batter into the skillet with a rubber spatula and level it out into an equal layer. Reduce the oven temperature to 400° Fahrenheit and return the skillet to the oven. Bake the cornbread for thirty minutes, or until it is golden brown, has a firm texture, and a toothpick pushed into the middle of the cake comes out clean.
4. Give the cornbread at least 10 minutes to cool down. Divide into wedges and serve at room temperature or heated. It's best eaten right out of the skillet. Kept leftovers in an airtight jar at room temperature for 3 days (toast before serving).

BRUSCHETTA CHICKEN

Prep Time: 15 Mins

Cook Time: 25 Mins

Total Time: 40 Mins

Servings: 6

INGREDIENTS

- 4 thin-cut boneless, skinless chicken breasts
- Kosher salt and freshly ground black pepper
- 2 tsp garlic powder
- 1 tbsp Italian seasoning
- 3 tbsp extra-virgin olive oil, divided
- 4 medium diced tomatoes
- ½ minced red onion
- 2 minced garlic cloves
- Balsamic vinegar, for finishing
- 13 cups of fresh chopped basil, plus additional leaves for garnish

- Grated Parmesan cheese, for finishing

INSTRUCTIONS

1. At first, season the chicken with salt, pepper, garlic powder, and Italian seasoning on both sides.
2. Now heat up 2 tbsp of the olive oil in a large skillet over medium heat. Then cook for 8-10 minutes, until the chicken is thoroughly browned on both sides and fully done.
3. Combine the remaining 1 tbsp olive oil, tomatoes, red onion, garlic, and basil in a bowl while the chicken cooks.
4. Place a large scoop of the tomato mixture on top of each chicken breast. Extra basil, balsamic vinegar, and Parmesan cheese can be added as garnish. Serve right away.

ICED SPICED SKILLET ROLLS

Total Time: 30 Mins

Servings: 1

INGREDIENTS

Rolls

- 2 tbsp. vegetable oil
- 1 cup of whole milk, warm
- 1/2 cup of granulated sugar
- 2 large eggs
- 1 tbsp. instant yeast
- 1 tsp. vanilla extract
- 1 tsp. salt
- 1/4 cup of plus 2 tbsp. butter, melted
- 4 1/4 cups of plus 1/4 cup all-purpose flour
- 1/2 cup of brown sugar
- 2 tbsp. ground cinnamon

Glaze

- 1/3 cup of confectioners' sugar
- 3 ounces softened cream cheese
- 3 tbsp. softened butter
- 1 tbsp. milk
- Pinch salt

INSTRUCTIONS

1. Make Rolls: Pour the oil into a large bowl. Mix milk, sugar, eggs, yeast, vanilla, salt, and 1/4 cup butter in a stand mixer on medium speed (with paddle attachment) until mixed. Mix in the flour until the dough comes together. Move using floured hands to a floured surface (dough will be very sticky). Make the dough until it is no longer sticky, adding up to 1/4 cup of extra flour as needed; shape the dough into a ball.
2. Transfer to a bowl and roll in the oil to coat. Cover with plastic wrap and a moist kitchen towel. Allow 2 hours to rise in a warm location.
3. Grease a 12-inch ovenproof skillet lightly. Punch dough down with greased hands and put out onto a lightly floured surface. Now roll out the dough into a 20" by 12" rectangle using a floured rolling pin. Sprinkle with brown sugar and cinnamon and brush with the remaining 2 tbsp butter. Begin rolling the dough tightly on one long side. Cut each piece into 12 pieces and put in a pan with swirling sides facing up. Cover with plastic wrap and a moist kitchen towel. Place in a warm location and allow to rise for 1 hour. Bake right away or keep refrigerated overnight. (If you refrigerated the cake, let it sit at room temperature for 30 minutes before baking.)
4. Preheat the oven to 350 degrees Fahrenheit. Uncover skillet and bake for 30 minutes, or until golden brown on top. Meanwhile, prepare the glaze: Combine all ingredients in a blender and blend until smooth. Take off

the pan from the oven and set it aside for 5 minutes. Finish with a glaze. Serve immediately.

Total Time: 20 Mins

Servings: 6

INGREDIENTS

- 1 large egg
- 2 tsp honey
- 2 cups of crushed Ritz crackers
- 1/2 tsp salt
- 1-1/2 pounds walleye fillets
- 1/3 to 1/2 cup of canola oil
- Optional: Minced fresh parsley and lemon wedge

INSTRUCTIONS

1. At first, beat the egg in a shallow bowl and add the honey. Combine crackers and salt in a small plate. Now dip the

fish in the egg mixture, then in the cracker mixture, turning to coat completely.

2. Cook fillets in oil in a cast-iron or other heavy pan over medium heat until brown and fish flakes readily with a fork, about 3-5 minutes each side. Serve with lemon wedges and parsley, if preferred.

ONE-PAN CREAMY CHICKEN FRICASSEE WITH SAGE

Prep Time: 15 Mins

Cook Time: 1 Hr 15 Mins

Total Time: 1 Hr 30 Mins

Servings: 6

INGREDIENTS

- 6 bone-in, skin-on chicken thighs
- 12 large sage leaves
- Kosher salt and freshly ground black pepper
- 2 tbsp extra-virgin olive oil
- 2 rosemary sprigs
- 2 garlic cloves, peeled and lightly crushed

- 4 slices of unsmoked bacon, roughly chopped
- 1 white onion, sliced into half-moons
- Scant ½ cup of white wine
- Generous ¾ cup of hot chicken stock (or hot water)
- 2 large egg yolks
- Juice of 1 lemon

INSTRUCTIONS

1. Remove the skin from each chicken thigh and insert a big sage leaf. Place the skin over the sage and replace it. Then season the chicken thighs with salt and pepper all over.

2. Heat the olive oil in a large, heavy-bottomed skillet with a lid over medium heat. Place them skin-side down chicken thighs in the pan with the rosemary and garlic—Cook for 15 to 20 minutes, or until the chicken skin is golden and crisp.

3. Turn the chicken thighs over and heat for another 5 minutes, or until the bacon is lightly browned and the onion is tender.

4. Allow the white wine to reduce for about 5 minutes before adding a third of the stock or hot water. Simmer, then turn the heat down to low and keep warm.

5. Cook for 30 to 40 minutes, slightly covered, until the flesh is cooked through and easily removed from the bone. To prevent the liquid from drying out throughout the cooking process, keep it topped up with the leftover stock or water. About one cup of liquid should remain in the pan for the sauce. Add the remaining six sage leaves to the pan 10 minutes before to the conclusion of cooking.

6. Now mix the egg yolks and lemon juice in a small bowl with a whisk. Place the chicken thighs on one side of the pan, allowing the fluids to pool on the other. Reduce the heat to a shallow setting. To thicken the sauce, gradually

add the egg mixture to the pan (you may not need to use all of it). To evenly spread the sauce, move the chicken about the pan. Serve right away.

SKIER'S SKILLET

Total Time: 30 Mins

Servings: 6

INGREDIENTS

- 12 ounces pork sausage links
- 5 medium peeled and quartered apples
- 3 tbsp brown sugar
- 1 tbsp lemon juice
- 1/8 tsp salt

INSTRUCTIONS

1. Cook sausages in a heavy 12-inch cast-iron or other ovenproof pan over medium-high heat for about 10 minutes, flipping periodically; drain. Add apple wedges to the mix. Brown sugar, lemon juice, and salt are

sprinkled on top. Cook, covered, for 10-15 minutes over medium heat, or until apples are soft and sausages are thoroughly cooked.

BALSAMIC CRANBERRY ROAST CHICKEN

Prep Time: 1 Hr 25 Mins

Cook Time: 35 Mins

Total Time: 2 Hr

Servings: 4

INGREDIENTS

- 2 cloves garlic
- ¼ cup of balsamic vinegar
- 1 tbsp soy sauce
- 3 tbsp extra-virgin olive oil
- 8 pieces chicken (thighs)
- 1½ cups of cranberries, divided
- Kosher salt and freshly ground black pepper
- Nonstick spray, as needed

- 1 tbsp chopped fresh thyme, with additional sprigs for garnish
- 1 tbsp fresh rosemary, plus additional sprigs for garnish

INSTRUCTIONS

1. Process the garlic, balsamic vinegar, olive oil, soy sauce, and 1/2 cup of the cranberries until smooth in the bowl of a food processor or blender.
2. Pour the marinade over the chicken in a big zip-top plastic bag. Now refrigerate for 30 minutes to 1 hour after closing the bag.
3. Preheat the oven to 375 degrees Fahrenheit. Grease a large oven-safe pan or casserole dish lightly with nonstick spray.
4. Reserving the marinade, remove the chicken from the bag. Rub the chicken with salt, pepper, thyme, and rosemary, then set the skin-side down in a skillet or dish. The remaining 1 cup cranberries should be strewn throughout the pan.
5. Roast the chicken for 20 to 25 minutes, or until the skin begins to brown and the flesh is nearly cooked through. Turn the chicken over and spray each piece with the remaining marinade. Remove the leftover marinade and toss it out.
6. Raise the oven temperature to 425° Fahrenheit and cook for another 5 to 8 minutes, or until the chicken skin is crispy. Serve right away.

SWEET POTATO KALE FRITTATA

Prep Time: 20 Mins

Cook Time: 10 Mins

Total Time: 30 Mins

Servings: 4

INGREDIENTS

- 6 large eggs
- 1 cup of half-and-half
- 1 tsp. Kosher salt
- 1/2 tsp. freshly ground pepper
- 2 cups of sweet potatoes
- 2 tbsp. olive oil
- 2 cups of firmly packed chopped kale

- 1/2 small red onion
- 2 garlic cloves
- 3 ounces goat cheese

INSTRUCTIONS

1. Preheat the oven to 350 degrees Fahrenheit. Combine the eggs and the following three ingredients.
2. Keep potatoes warm. In a 10-inch ovenproof nonstick pan, heat 1 tbsp of oil over medium heat and sauté sweet potatoes for 8-10 minutes, or until they are tender and golden. Sauté kale and next two ingredients in remaining 1 tbsp oil for 3 to 4 minutes, or until kale is wilted and tender; toss in potatoes. Cook for another 3 minutes after pouring the egg mixture equally over the veggies. Goat cheese should be sprinkled over the egg mixture.
3. Bake for 10 to 14 minutes at 350 degrees Fahrenheit, or until set.

CRUSTED SALMON

Prep Time: 15 Mins

Bake Time: 10 Mins

Total Time: 25 Mins

Servings: 4

INGREDIENTS

- 4 salmon fillets (about 6 ounces each)
- 1 cup of 2% milk
- 1 cup of finely chopped pecans
- 1/4 cup of all-purpose flour
- 2 tbsp packed brown sugar
- 1 tsp seasoned salt
- 1 tsp pepper

- 3 tbsp canola oil

INSTRUCTIONS

1. Fill a small dish halfway with milk and add the salmon fillets. Coat on the other side. Drain after ten minutes of letting it settle.
2. Meanwhile, mix the pecans, flour, brown sugar, seasoned salt, and pepper in a small bowl. Coat the fish fillets with the pecan mixture and gently press it into the flesh.
3. Brown salmon in oil in a large cast-iron or other ovenproof pan over medium-high heat. Preheat oven to 400° Fahrenheit and bake for 8-10 minutes, or until salmon begins to flake easily with a fork.

WHITE WINE COQ AU VIN

Prep Time: 15 Mins

Cook Time: 40 Mins

Total Time: 55 Mins

Servings: 6

INGREDIENTS

- 3 pounds chicken (8 pieces—thighs, breasts and drumsticks)
- Kosher salt and freshly ground black pepper
- 2 tbsp unsalted butter
- 4 strips diced bacon
- 1 large diced sweet onion
- 3 minced garlic cloves

- 1 pint sliced cremini mushrooms
- 2 cups of dry white wine
- 1 tbsp whole-grain mustard
- ½ cup of heavy cream
- ¼ cup of chopped fresh parsley

INSTRUCTIONS

1. Add salt and pepper to the chicken. Melt the butter in a large pan over medium heat. Cook the chicken in the skillet until it's thoroughly browned on both sides, about 4 minutes each side.
2. Take off the chicken from the skillet and place it on a plate to cool. Cook the bacon in the pan for 3 minutes, or until the fat begins to render.
3. After that, add the onion and cook for 5 minutes, or until it becomes translucent. Sauté the garlic and mushrooms for 5 to 6 minutes, or until the mushrooms are soft.
4. Return the browned chicken to the pan. Pour the wine into the skillet, toss in the mustard, and set the heat to medium-low to bring the mixture to a simmer.
5. Now cover the skillet and cook for 15 to 20 minutes, or until the chicken is almost done.
6. Take off the lid from the skillet and pour in the cream. Simmer for 8 to 10 minutes, or until the sauce thickens and the chicken is thoroughly cooked.
7. Serve immediately with a parsley garnish.

SKILLET SHRIMP, SAUSAGE, AND RICE

Prep Time: 15 Mins

Cook Time: 20 Mins

Total Time: 35 Mins

Servings: 4

INGREDIENTS

- 2 tbsp. olive oil
- 6 ounces fully cooked andouille sausage
- 1 medium onion
- 1 red pepper
- 2 clove garlic
- 1 cup of long-grain white rice
- 1/2 cup of dry white wine

- 2 tsp. Creole seasoning
- 1 3/4 cup of low-sodium chicken broth
- 12 ounces peeled and deveined shrimp
- 12 ounces plum tomatoes
- 1/2 cup of fresh flat-leaf parsley

INSTRUCTIONS

1. Add oil and heat the oil in a large skillet on medium-high heat. Cook, stirring occasionally, until the sausage is browned, about 1 to 2 minutes each side; remove to a platter.
2. After that, decrease the heat to medium, add the onion, and simmer, covered, for 4 minutes, stirring periodically. Add the pepper and garlic and simmer, turning regularly, for another 5 minutes, or until the veggies are just soft.
3. Bring to a simmer after adding the rice, wine, and spices. Bring the broth to a boil, then remove from the heat. Decrease the heat to low and cover for twelve minutes.
4. Fold the sausage into the rice mixture, then nestle the shrimp in the partly cooked rice and simmer, covered, for another 4 to 5 minutes, or until the shrimp are opaque throughout and the rice is soft. Before serving, fold in the tomatoes and garnish with parsley.

STEAK WITH CREAMY MUSHROOMS AND SPINACH

Total Time: 35 Mins

Servings: 4

INGREDIENTS

- 2 (12-ounce) strip steaks, 1 1/2 inches thick each
- Kosher salt and freshly ground black pepper
- 3 tbsp. olive oil, divided
- 4 cloves skin-on garlic, plus
- 2 finely chopped cloves, divided
- 1 sprig of rosemary, plus
- 1 tsp chopped rosemary, divided
- 12 ounces assorted mushrooms, quartered

- 1 tbsp. Dijon mustard
- 1/2 cup of dry white wine
- 1 bunch roughly chopped spinach, thick stems discarded, and leaves
- 1/2 cup of crème fraîche or sour cream

INSTRUCTIONS

1. Preheat the oven to 425 degrees Fahrenheit. Flavor the meat with salt and pepper before serving. Over medium-high heat, heat a medium-size cast-iron pan. Add 1 tbsp oil. Add the steak, skin-on garlic cloves, and rosemary sprig to the pan. Cook for 4 to 8 minutes, rotating once until browned.
2. Place pan in oven and roast until the desired doneness is reached, about 3 to 6 minutes for medium. Now transfer the steaks to a chopping board and set them aside for at least 10 minutes before slicing.
3. Come back the skillet to a medium-high heat setting (make sure to keep an oven mitt on the handle). Add the mushrooms and the remaining 2 tbsp of oil to the pan. Season with salt and pepper. Then cook, occasionally stirring, for 6-8 minutes, or until softened and beginning to brown. Cook, constantly stirring, for 1 minute, until the garlic and rosemary are fragrant.
4. Mix in the mustard and the wine. Cook for 30 seconds, stirring constantly. Placing the mushrooms on a platter is a good idea. Cook, stirring, for 1 to 2 minutes, or until spinach begins to wilt. Take off from heat and mix in the mushroom and crème fraîche. Salt and pepper to taste. Garnish with thinly cut steaks.

Prep Time: 25 Mins

Cook Time: 35 Mins

Total Time:1 Hr

Servings: 4

INGREDIENTS

- 10 small new yellow potatoes
- 2 tbsp. olive oil
- 4 small chicken legs
- Kosher salt

- Pepper
- 6 clove garlic
- 2 small red onions
- 1 large red pepper
- 1 tbsp. chopped fresh rosemary
- 2 sprig rosemary
- 5 medium carrots

INSTRUCTIONS

1. Preheat the oven to 425 degrees Fahrenheit. Place the potatoes on a platter that can be microwaved—now microwave for 10 minutes on high. After cool enough to handle, cut in half and lay away.
2. In a large oven-safe skillet, heat 1 tbsp oil over medium heat. Sprinkle the chicken with a half tsp each of salt and pepper, then cook it with the skin side down for eight to ten minutes, or until the skin is golden and crisp. Place them skin-side down on a platter.
3. Cook, stirring, for 2 minutes with the remaining tbsp of oil, garlic, onions, red pepper, and chopped rosemary in the skillet. Toss in the potatoes and carrots, seasoning with 1/4 tsp each of salt and pepper.
4. Now place the chicken in the middle of the veggies in the skillet. Sprinkle the rosemary sprigs on top and roast for 30 to 35 minutes until the chicken is done and the vegetables are soft and golden brown.

GREEK CHICKEN AND RICE SKILLET

Prep Time: 15 Mins

Cook Time: 25 Mins

Total Time: 40 Mins

Servings: 6

INGREDIENTS

- 6 chicken thighs
- Kosher salt and freshly ground black pepper
- 1 tsp dried oregano
- 1 tsp garlic powder

- 3 lemons
- 2 tbsp extra-virgin olive oil
- ½ minced red onion
- 2 minced garlic cloves
- 1 cup of long-grain rice
- 2½ cups of chicken broth
- 1 tbsp chopped fresh oregano, plus more for garnishing
- 1 cup of green olives
- ½ cup of crumbled feta cheese
- ⅓ cup of fresh chopped fresh parsley

INSTRUCTIONS

1. Preheat the oven to 375 degrees Fahrenheit. Prepare the chicken thighs by seasoning them with salt and pepper. Combine the dried oregano, garlic powder, and 1 lemon zest in a small bowl. Apply the mixture on the chicken in an equal layer.
2. In a large oven-safe skillet, heat the olive oil over medium heat. Sear the chicken, skin side down, for 7 to 9 minutes, until it is thoroughly browned. Transfer to a platter and set aside.
3. In a large pan, sauté the onion and garlic until transparent, about 5 minutes. Season with salt and stir in the rice. Cook for 1 minute.
4. Bring the mixture to a low boil with the chicken broth. Add the fresh oregano and lemon juice and mix well. Set aside the remaining 2 lemons after slicing them.
5. Place the chicken in the rice mixture, skin side up. Toss the chicken and rice together in a pan and bake for 20-25 minutes, or until the rice is done and the chicken is no longer pink.

6. Place the chicken under the broiler and top with lemon wedges. Broil the skillet for 3 minutes, or until the lemons are gently charred and the chicken skin is crisp.

7. Serve immediately with the olives and feta cheese in the pan, garnished with fresh parsley.

CAST-IRON HASSELBACK POTATOES

Total Time: 1 Hr

Servings: 6

INGREDIENTS

- 5 tbsp. unsalted butter, melted and divided, plus more for pan
- 6 medium russet or Yukon Gold potatoes

3 tbsp. divided M5 Spice Rub

- 3 tbsp. chopped fresh flat-leaf parsley
- Sour cream, for serving

INSTRUCTIONS

1. Preheat the oven to 425 degrees Fahrenheit. Distribute butter on the bottom and sides of a cast-iron pan about 12 inches in diameter. Cut each potato crosswise into 1/8-inch-thick slices, keeping approximately 1/4 inch of potato intact, without cutting all the way through to the bottom (this will help them hold together). Arrange potatoes 1 inch apart in pan. Apply 2 1/2 tsp of butter. Add 1 tsp of spice rub.
2. Bake for 30 minutes with the pan covered with aluminum foil. Remove the foil and sprinkle the remaining 2 1/2 tsp butter and 1 tsp spice rub over the potatoes (which should have opened up somewhat). Bake for 15-20 minutes, uncovered, until potatoes are crispy on the outside and soft in the interior. Serve with parsley as a garnish. Serve alongside a spoonful of sour cream.

Total Time: 35 Mins

Servings: 6

INGREDIENTS

- 2 slices bacon, cut into 1/4-in. pieces
- 1 small peeled and finely chopped onion
- 2 minced garlic cloves

- 2 large bunches of mustard greens (each weighing about 1 pound), stems removed, and leaves ripped
- 3 tbsp. fresh lemon juice
- 3 large egg yolks plus
- 6 large eggs, split
- Kosher salt and pepper
- 6 tbsp. melted unsalted butter
- 1 tbsp. fresh chopped tarragon plus more for garnish
- Crusty bread for serving

INSTRUCTIONS

1. Preheat the oven to 400 degrees Fahrenheit. Then place bacon in a large pan and fry for 5 minutes over medium-low heat. Cook, occasionally stirring, until onion is barely soft, about 6 to 8 minutes. Then Sauté for one minute after adding the garlic.

2. Add greens in three batches, tossing and rotating each batch until wilted, about 3 minutes. Now season with a quarter tsp of salt and pepper, then remove from fire. Make six wells in the greens and place 1 entire egg in each. Bake for 10 to 12 minutes, or until the whites are set, and the yolks are the proper consistency.

3. Meanwhile, in a blender, combine the egg yolks, lemon juice, and 1/4 tsp salt for 5 seconds on high. Pour in the melted butter gently while the blender is running. Half of the hollandaise should be spooned over the eggs, sprinkled with tarragon, and served with toast and the remaining hollandaise if preferred.

SKILLET SPINACH-ARTICHOKE DIP WITH FIRE-ROASTED BREAD

Total Time: 45 Mins

Servings: 6

INGREDIENTS

- Canola oil, for grill grate
- 8-ounce pack of cream cheese, at room temperature

- 1/2 cup of sour cream
- 3 ounces grated Parmesan
- 1 tsp. lemon zest, plus 3 tbsp lemon juice
- 1 large, pressed garlic clove
- Kosher salt and freshly ground black pepper
- 14-ounce can of drained and chopped artichokes
- 10-ounce pack of frozen leaf spinach, thawed and squeezed dry
- 1 small, sliced loaf of country bread
- 3 tbsp olive oil

INSTRUCTIONS

1. Heat the grill to medium for both direct and indirect grilling. Clean and gently grease grates with canola oil while they're hot.
2. Combine cream cheese, sour cream, 1/4 cup Parmesan, lemon zest and juice, and garlic in a mixing bowl. Salt & pepper to taste. Fold in the artichokes and spinach. Transfer to a cast-iron skillet with a 9-inch diameter. Finish with the remaining 1/4 cup Parmesan cheese. Wrap aluminum foil around the dish.
3. Cook, covered, for 10 minutes over indirect heat in a skillet. Remove the foil and flip the skillet over low heat. Cook for 18-20 minutes, uncovered, or until bubbling and golden brown. Remove the grill from the heat.
4. Drizzle olive oil over the bread. Grill for 20 to 30 seconds over direct heat, rotating periodically until crisp. Serve with a side of dip.

Prep Time: 40 Mins

Cook Time: 50 Mins

Total Time: 1 Hr 30 Mins

Servings: 4

INGREDIENTS

- 4 bone-in, skin-on chicken breast halves
- Salt and freshly cracked pepper
- 2 tbsp grapeseed oil
- 4 tbsp unsalted butter, divided
- 10 shallots, peeled, larger ones halved lengthwise
- 4 smashed and roughly chopped garlic cloves
- 8-10 sprigs fresh thyme, divided
- ½ cup of dry white wine
- 1½ cups of low-sodium chicken stock
- 8 Medjool dates, pitted and halved lengthwise
- ⅔ cup smashed and pitted green olives
- 1½ tbsp apple cider vinegar
- 1 lemon, zested and juiced

INSTRUCTIONS

1. Before cooking, let the chicken rest for 30 minutes at room temperature.
2. Preheat the oven to 450 degrees Fahrenheit. Put a rack in the oven's top third.
3. Put the biggest cast-iron skillet in the oven for fifteen minutes. Dry the chicken breasts and season them thoroughly on all sides with salt and pepper. Take off the heated skillet from the oven with care and set it on the stovetop. Put the grapeseed oil in the pan and heat it over medium heat until you see a small ripple. The oil should be quite hot.
4. Cook the chicken, skin side down, in two batches until the skin is crispy and golden brown, 4 to 5 minutes. Remove all except one tbsp of the oil from the pan.
5. As you make your sauce, remove the chicken from the skillet and place it on a platter. Dissolve two tbsp butter in a pan over medium heat and add the onions. Cook the

shallots, stirring occasionally, for 5 to 6 minutes, or until caramelized and brown. Sprinkle with salt and add the garlic, a few thyme sprigs, and 1 tbsp of butter. Cook, tossing frequently, until the shallots begin to soften, about 5 to 7 minutes. Reduce the wine by half after deglazing the pan. Add the stock and a couple more thyme sprigs. Simmer the sauce for 15 minutes over medium to low heat, until it has slightly reduced. Check for seasoning before adding the dates and olives to the sauce.

6. Return the skin-side up chicken breasts to the pan and bake in the oven. Roast the chicken for about twenty minutes, or until it's just cooked through. The temperature should read 160° Fahrenheit on an instant-read thermometer put into the thickest area of the breast.

7. Now place the chicken breasts on a platter and cover with foil to keep warm. Return the skillet to the stovetop over low to medium heat and stir in the vinegar. Now simmer for 3-5 minutes, or until the sauce is thick enough to coat the back of a wooden spoon. Take off it from the fire and whisk in the lemon juice and the remaining 1 tbsp butter. Seasoning should be checked and adjusted if necessary.

8. Return the chicken to the pan and garnish with the remaining thyme and lemon zest before serving.

Total Time:1 Hr 10 Mins

Servings: 8

INGREDIENTS

- 4 tbsp divided olive oil
- 1 pound large, peeled and deveined shrimp
- 8 ounces sliced Spanish chorizo
- 1 large chopped onion
- 2 large yellow or red bell peppers, cut into quarters and sliced into thin strips
- 2 tsp. finely crushed saffron threads
- Kosher salt and freshly ground black pepper
- 3 chopped garlic cloves
- 2 cups of short-grain rice
- 1 tsp smoked paprika
- 1/2 cup of dry white wine
- 4 cups of chicken stock
- 2 tsp lemon zest, plus
- 6 tbsp liquid and serving wedges
- 16 mussels
- 1/2 cup of pitted green olives, cracked
- 1/2 cup roughly chopped fresh flat-leaf parsley

INSTRUCTIONS

1. Warm 1 tbsp oil in a 12-inch cast-iron pan on medium-high. Cook, rotating once, for 2 to 4 minutes, or until shrimp are browned; transfer to a dish. Lower the heat down to a low level. Then combine the chorizo and 1 tbsp of oil in a pan. Cook for 2 minutes, often stirring, or until

the chorizo begins to crisp and release its oils. Half the chorizo should be placed on a dish.

2. Increase the heat to medium. Add the onion, bell pepper, saffron, and the remaining 2 tbsp oil. Season with salt and pepper to taste. Now cook for 5-6 minutes, stirring occasionally, or until soft. Cook for 1 minute, stirring regularly, or until garlic is fragrant. Mix in the rice and paprika. Cook for 1 minute, stirring regularly, or until rice is thoroughly coated.

3. Cook for 30 seconds, or until nearly all of the wine has evaporated. Pour in the broth and three tbsp of lemon juice. Cook for 4 to 6 minutes, stirring often, or until rice begins to absorb liquid. Cook on low heat for 18 to 20 minutes, or until most of the liquid is absorbed.

4. Put the shrimp and mussels in the pan, hinge points down. Cook for 5 to 6 minutes, covered, or until mussels open, shrimp become pink, and rice is tender.

5. Take off the pan from heat and add the olives, chorizo, and the remaining 3 tbsp lemon juice. Allow for a 5-minute break. On top, lemon zest and parsley are sprinkled. On the side, lemon slices.

Prep Time: 15 Mins

Cook Time: 25 Mins

Total Time: 40 Mins

Servings: 4

INGREDIENTS

- 1 tbsp. extra-virgin olive oil
- 5-ounce container of coarsely chopped baby spinach
- 3 chopped garlic cloves
- 1/2 cup of ricotta
- 1 1/2 ounces grated Parmesan
- 1 tbsp fresh lemon juice
- 1/4 tsp. crush red pepper flakes
- Kosher salt
- Freshly ground black pepper
- 1 1/2 tbsp cornmeal
- 1 pound room temperature store-bought pizza dough
- 6 ounces Fontina cheese, grated
- 14-ounce can drain and quartered artichoke hearts
- Fresh basil leaves, torn, for serving

INSTRUCTIONS

1. Set the oven temperature to 450° Fahrenheit and place the lowest rack in the oven. In a 10-inch pan, heat the oil "medium-high heat in a skillet. Cook, occasionally stirring, until the spinach has wilted and the liquid has evaporated, 3 to 4 minutes; remove to a platter. Allow the skillet to cool somewhat before wiping clean.

2. Combine the ricotta, Parmesan, lemon juice, and red pepper flakes in a bowl. Salt and black pepper to taste. Coat the skillet with cornmeal. Stretch the dough into a 12-inch ring "in a circle. Carefully push the dough into the skillet's bottom and up the sides.

3. Arrange the ricotta mixture, spinach, Fontina, and artichokes on top of the dough. Cook for 20-24 minutes, or until the crust is golden brown. Allow for a 5-minute rest period.

4. Cut into wedges and dusted with basil.

Prep Time: 10 Mins

Cook Time: 7 Mins

Total Time: 17 Mins

Servings: 2

INGREDIENTS

- 2 fresh salmon filet's (see notes)
- Kosher salt
- Cracked black pepper
- Pompeian Avocado oil Spray
- 1 cup of small cherry tomatoes halved
- 2 tbsp fresh chopped tarragon
- 1 tbsp unsalted butter

INSTRUCTIONS

1. Preheat oven to 450 degrees Fahrenheit.
2. Using the avocado oil spray, lightly coat the fish.
3. Salt and black pepper to taste.
4. Preheat an ovenproof pan large enough to hold both pieces of salmon for about 1 minute over high heat.
5. Spray the pan liberally with the avocado oil spray.
6. Place the salmon skin side up in the pan and sear for 1 minute.
7. Carefully flip the salmon over onto the skin side with a spatula.
8. Arrange the tomatoes around the fish and top with the tarragon.
9. Finally, add two slices of butter to each side of the pan.

10. Preheat the oven to 375° Fahrenheit and bake the pan for 7-8 minutes.

I used fish that was approximately 2 inches broad and 1 1/2 inches tall. Your salmon will cook faster if it is thinner. Rather of buying at the end, try to buy from the middle. Gently touch the thickest area with your finger to see whether it's ready; it should feel somewhat hard. It will cook quickly and continue to cook after you remove it from the oven. It's usually best to remove it from the oven early and avoid overcooking it.

Prep Time: 20 Mins

Cook Time: 25 Mins

Total Time: 55 Mins

Servings: 4

INGREDIENTS

- 2 tbsp extra-virgin olive oil
- 1 minced onion
- 2 minced cloves garlic
- 1 seeded and minced jalapeño
- 1 pound spinach (thawed if frozen)
- 1 tsp dried cumin
- ¾ tsp coriander
- Salt and freshly ground black pepper
- 2 tbsp harissa
- ½ cup of vegetable broth
- 8 large eggs
- Chopped fresh parsley, as needed for serving
- Chopped fresh cilantro, as needed for serving
- Red-pepper flakes, as needed for serving

INSTRUCTIONS

1. Preheat the oven to 350 degrees Fahrenheit.
2. Add the olive oil in a large oven-safe skillet and heat over medium heat. Add the onion and cook for 4 to 5 minutes,

or until soft. Sauté for 1 minute more after adding the garlic and jalapeno.

3. Stir in the spinach and simmer until thoroughly wilted, 4 to 5 minutes if using fresh spinach, or until cooked through, 1 to 2 minutes if using frozen spinach.

4. Cumin, coriander, salt, pepper, and harissa are used to season the dish. Cook for one minute, or until the mixture is fragrant.

5. Puree the ingredients in the bowl of a food processor or in a blender until it is coarse. Puree in the broth until it is thick and smooth.

6. Remove the skillet from the oven and coat it with nonstick cooking spray. Return the spinach mixture to the pan and create eight circular wells with a wooden spoon.

7. Crack the eggs gently into the wells. Place the skillet to the oven and cook for 20 to 25 minutes or until the egg whites are totally set but the yolks are still somewhat jiggly.

8. To taste, top the shakshuka with parsley, cilantro, and red pepper flakes. Serve right away.

Prep Time: 15 Mins

Cook Time: 40 Mins

Total Time: 55 Mins

Servings: 10

INGREDIENTS

- 2 tbsp vegetable oil
- 1 cup of stone-ground yellow cornmeal
- 1/2 cup of all-purpose flour
- 2 tbsp sugar
- 2 tsp baking powder
- 1 tsp salt
- 1/2 tsp Freshly ground pepper
- 3 cups of fresh yellow corn kernels
- 1 small jalapeño
- 1 1/4 cups of Buttermilk
- 1 cup of cream
- 3 large eggs
- 1 can mild green chiles

INSTRUCTIONS

1. Preheat the oven to 375 degrees Fahrenheit. Put an oil-covered 10-inch cast-iron pan in the oven. In a large bowl, combine cornmeal and the following 5 ingredients; stir in corn and jalapenos. In the center of the mixture, make a well. Combine buttermilk and the next three

ingredients in a mixing bowl. Stir until the dry ingredients are moistened before adding the buttermilk liquid to the cornmeal mixture. Pour into a pan that has already been heated.

2. Preheat oven to 375° Fahrenheit and bake for 40–45 minutes, or until golden brown and firm.

Prep Time: 10 Mins

Cook Time: 20 Mins

Total Time: 30 Mins

Servings: 4

INGREDIENTS

Taco Cauliflower Rice Skillet

- 16 ounces extra lean ground turkey or chicken
- 1/2 diced yellow onion
- 1/2 diced red bell pepper
- 1/2 diced green bell pepper
- 1-ounce packets taco seasoning
- 15 ounce can of diced tomatoes drained
- 4 ounces can dice green chiles drained
- 12 ounces bag of frozen cauliflower rice
- 1/2 cup of chicken broth
- Salt to taste

Optional Additions

- Shredded cheese
- Non-fat plain Greek yogurt
- Avocado
- Pico de Gallo
- Tortilla Chips

INSTRUCTIONS

1. First, warm the oil in a large nonstick skillet over medium-high heat.
2. Cooking sprays the ground beef, onion, bell peppers, and taco seasoning together.
3. Cook, breaking up the meat for approximately 10 minutes, or until the meat is cooked through.
4. Stir in the tomatoes, green chiles, rice, and broth after the rice is done cooking.
5. Now cook for 5-10 minutes, or until well heated.
6. Taste and season with salt to taste, then serve with your choice of optional condiments!

NOTES

Make your own taco seasoning with the help of this recipe for Homemade Taco Seasoning if you don't already have some on hand.

SKILLET STEAK WITH ASPARAGUS AND POTATOES

Prep Time: 10 Mins

Cook Time: 50 Mins

Total Time: 1 Hr

Servings: 2

INGREDIENTS

- ½ pound baby red potatoes halved
- ¼ cup of extra-virgin olive oil, divided
- Salt and freshly ground black pepper
- 1 asparagus bunch, sliced into bite-size portions
- 1 tsp smoked paprika
- 1 tsp garlic powder
- 1½ pounds sirloin or strip steak

Herb Sauce

- Zest and juice of 1 lemon
- ¼ cup of finely chopped fresh parsley
- 2 tbsp finely chopped fresh mint
- 1 smashed garlic clove
- Salt and freshly ground black pepper
- 1 pinch of red pepper flakes
- 2 tbsp extra-virgin olive oil

INSTRUCTIONS

1. Preheat the oven to 400 degrees Fahrenheit.
2. Cook the steak as follows: Toss the potatoes with 2 tbsp olive oil in a large oven-safe pan and season with salt and pepper. Roast the potatoes in the oven for 15 to 17 minutes, or until they are just starting to get soft.
3. Drizzle 1 tbsp additional oil into the pan with the asparagus—roast for another 12 to 15 minutes, or until the veggies are soft. Now remove the veggies from the pan and put them aside. Reduce the oven temperature to 350 degrees Fahrenheit.
4. Coat the steak with the remaining 1 tbsp olive oil on both sides. Add the smoked paprika, garlic powder, salt, and pepper to taste.
5. Grill the steak on both sides in a hot pan for 4-5 minutes each side (If necessary, heat the pan over medium heat on the stovetop). Cook the steak in the oven until it achieves the desired doneness, about 10 to 12 minutes more for medium-rare.
6. Rest the steak for 15 minutes after removing it from the pan.
7. To make the herb sauce: Mix the lemon zest, lemon juice, parsley, mint, garlic, salt, crushed red pepper flakes, pepper, and olive oil in a small bowl.
8. Slice the meat thinly and serve with the sauce on top of the potatoes and asparagus. Serve right away.

CAST-IRON APPLE-BLACKBERRY CRUMBLE WITH SOUR CREAM WHIP

Total Time: 1 Hr 45 Mins

Servings: 10

INGREDIENTS

Crumb Topping

- 3/4 cup of all-purpose flour, leveled with a spoon
- 1/2 cup of packed brown sugar
- 3 tbsp granulated sugar
- 1 tsp ground cinnamon
- 1/4 tsp ground cardamom
- 1/2 tsp kosher salt
- 8 tbsp of cold unsalted butter, cubed
- 1 cup of old-fashioned rolled oats
- 3/4 cup of chopped pecans

Apple-Blackberry Filling

- Unsalted butter, for pan
- 4 pounds of apples, prepared by peeling, coring, and slicing to a thickness of half an inch
- 2 cups of blackberries
- 2/3 cup of granulated sugar
- 3 tbsp. cornstarch
- 1 tbsp lemon zest and 2 tbsp fresh lemon juice
- 3/4 tsp kosher salt

Sour Cream Whip

- 1 cup of heavy cream
- 1 cup of sour cream
- 1/4 cup of confectioners' sugar
- 1 tsp pure vanilla extract

INSTRUCTIONS

1. Stir together the flour, brown sugar, granulated sugar, cinnamon, cardamom, and salt in a large bowl. Then add butter and use a pastry blender or your fingertips to chop it into the flour until the mixture resembles coarse meal. Mix in the oats and pecans, forming tiny clumps. While making the filling, place it in the freezer.
2. Preheat the oven to 375 degrees Fahrenheit. Butter a 12-inch cast-iron skillet that is shallow. Combine apples, blackberries, sugar, cornstarch, the zest and juice of one lemon, and salt in a bowl. Transfer to the skillet that has been prepared. Toss the topping on top of the fruit.
3. Bake them for 50 minutes to an hour, or until the topping has browned and the fruit has begun to bubble (cover with foil after 20 minutes if crumble becomes too dark before fruit is bubbling). Wait 10 minutes before serving on a wire rack to cool down. Serve with a side of Sour Cream Whip.
4. To make the Sour Cream Whip, beat heavy cream, sour cream, confectioners' sugar, and pure vanilla extract together with an electric mixer on medium speed for 1 to 2 minutes, or until soft peaks form. Approximately 1 1/2 cup.

CAULIFLOWER AND CHICKPEA MASALA

Prep Time: 10 Mins

Cook Time: 30 Mins

Total Time: 40 Mins

Servings: 4

INGREDIENTS

Masala Spice Mix

- 2 tbsp garam masala
- 1/2 tsp cumin
- 1/2 tsp turmeric
- 1/2 tsp smoked paprika
- 1/4 tsp cayenne
- 1/2 tsp salt
- Freshly Cracked Pepper

Skillet Ingredients

- 1 yellow onion
- 3 garlic cloves
- 1/2 tbsp grated fresh ginger
- 2 tbsp olive oil
- 12 ounces frozen cauliflower florets
- 15 ounces can drained chickpeas
- 15 ounces can tomato sauce
- 1/4 cup of water

- 1/3 cup of heavy cream
- Salt to taste

INSTRUCTIONS

1. Combine the ingredients for the masala spice mix in a small bowl (garam masala, cumin, turmeric, smoked paprika, cayenne, salt, and pepper).
2. Now finely dice the onion, garlic, and ginger, and grate the ginger. Pour olive oil into a large pan and add the three ingredients. Sauté on medium heat until the onions are brown and tender (about 3 minutes). Continue to sauté for another minute after adding the spice blend.
3. Add the frozen cauliflower florets to the pan with the aromatics and spices, and continue to sauté for approximately 5 minutes, or until the cauliflower is thoroughly thawed and covered with spices.
4. In a pan, combine the drained chickpeas, tomato sauce, and 1/4 cup water. Stir to incorporate, then cook, stirring regularly, for about 15 minutes over medium-low heat. This will assist the tomato sauce's acidity to be mellowed and the spices to mix. Add a couple additional tbsp of water if the mixture gets too dry while it simmers.
5. After the sauce has simmered for fifteen minutes, remove it from the heat and stir in the heavy cream. Taste the masala and season with salt if required. Serve over rice or with a slice of bread for dipping in a bowl.

Prep Time: 20 Mins

Cook Time: 15 Mins

Total Time: 35 Mins

Servings: 6

INGREDIENTS

- 3 ears of corn on the cob
- 2 tbsp melted butter
- 1 pound lasagna noodles, roughly broken
- Kosher salt and freshly ground black pepper
- 4 tbsp extra-virgin olive oil, divided
- 1 pint of cherry tomatoes
- 2 large zucchini ribbons (peeled using a vegetable peeler)
- ½ cup of grated Parmesan cheese
- 1 bunch of asparagus, peeled with a vegetable peeler into ribbons
- ¼ cup of capers
- 3 tbsp chopped fresh basil

INSTRUCTIONS

1. Warm a large skillet over medium heat. Add the corn to the pan after brushing it with the melted butter. Sear for

approximately 4 minutes per side, or until nicely charred. Allow cooling somewhat before removing the kernels from the cob.

2. After that, cook the lasagna noodles in a big pot of salted water for approximately 7 to 9 minutes, or until they're just tender enough to eat.

3. After rinsing the noodles, toss them with 2 tbsp of olive oil. Fry the remaining corn in the same skillet you used to heat up some of your leftover olive oil.

4. Now season the tomatoes with salt and pepper in the skillet. Cook for

1. 6-7 minutes, or until the tomatoes have popped. Cook until the zucchini and asparagus are soft, about 4 minutes.

5. Toss the noodles and corn together in the skillet. Toss in the Parmesan, capers, and basil until well combined. Serve right away

SKILLET CHICKEN WITH BRUSSELS SPROUTS AND APPLES

Total Time: 20 Mins

Servings: 4

INGREDIENTS

- 1 1/2 pounds of chicken thighs without skin or bones
- 2 tsp chopped fresh thyme
- Kosher salt and black pepper
- 1 tbsp canola oil
- 12-ounce shredded Brussels sprouts
- 1 sliced apple
- 1/2 sliced red onion
- 1 chopped garlic clove
- 2 tbsp white balsamic vinegar
- 2 tsp brown sugar
- 1/3 cup of chopped toasted pecans

INSTRUCTIONS

1. Add fresh thyme, kosher salt, and black pepper to chicken thighs. Cook until cooked through in a large pan with canola oil over medium-high heat, 4 to 5 minutes per side; remove to a dish.
2. Add shredded Brussels sprouts, apple, red onion, and a clove of garlic to a pan. Then cook for 5-6 minutes,

stirring periodically, or until Brussels sprouts are wilted and onion is softened. Combine the white balsamic vinegar and brown sugar in a bowl. Season with black pepper and kosher salt.

3. Finally, come back the chicken to the pan and sprinkle the toasted nuts on top.

Prep Time: 25 Mins

Cook Time: 30 Mins

Total Time: 55 Mins

Servings: 4

INGREDIENTS

- 3tsp. canola oil
- 8 small bone-in, skin-on chicken thighs
- 1/2 medium chopped onion
- 3 chopped garlic cloves,
- 1 1/2 tsp. smoked paprika
- 1/2 tsp. ground cumin
- 1 pt. grape tomatoes
- 2 15-ounce cans rinsed chickpeas
- Fresh thyme leaves, for serving
- Kosher salt and freshly ground black pepper
- 1/2 cup of plain Greek yogurt

INSTRUCTIONS

1. Preheat the oven to 425 degrees Fahrenheit. Then warm the oil in a large ovenproof skillet over medium-high

heat. Garnish the chicken with salt and pepper before serving. In batches, cook until the skin is browned and crispy, 8 to 10 minutes. Remove the chicken to a platter and set aside the skillet.

2. Then add the onion and garlic to the same skillet and sauté, rotating occasionally, until they begin to soften, about 2-4 minutes. Cook, stirring constantly, for 30 seconds, until paprika and cumin are aromatic. Bring to a simmer with the tomatoes and chickpeas. Salt & pepper to taste. Put the chicken in the mixture, skin side up.

3. Roast for 20 to 25 minutes, or until the internal temperature of the chicken reaches 165° Fahrenheit.

4. Serve with yogurt and fresh thyme leaves on the side.

Prep Time: 20 Mins

Bake Time: 15 Mins

Total Time: 35 Mins

Servings: 8

INGREDIENTS

- 2 cups of all-purpose flour
- 3 tsp baking powder
- 1/2 tsp baking soda
- 1/4 tsp salt
- 3 tbsp cold butter
- 3/4 to 1 cup of buttermilk
- 1 tbsp fat-free milk

INSTRUCTIONS

1. Preheat the oven to 450 degrees Fahrenheit. Then combine the flour, baking powder, baking soda, and salt in a large bowl; add the butter and continue to chop until the mixture resembles coarse crumbs. Add just enough buttermilk to moisten the dough.

2. Now knead the dough 3-4 times on a lightly floured surface. Pat or roll to a thickness of 3/4 inch. Use a

floured 2-1/2-inch biscuit cutter to cut the biscuits. Place in a big cast-iron or other ovenproof pan that hasn't been oiled.

3. Brush the surface with milk. Bake until golden, 12 to 15 minutes.

CRISPY CHICKEN THIGHS WITH PEPPERS & SALSA VERDE

Total Time: 20 Mins

Servings: 4

INGREDIENTS

- 1 1/4 cups of low-sodium chicken broth
- 1 box roasted garlic-and-olive oil couscous
- 2 tsp vegetable oil
- 6 large skin-on, bone-in chicken thighs
- 1 1/2 tsp Kosher salt
- 3/4 tsp Freshly ground pepper
- 3 medium colorful bell peppers
- 1/2 medium sweet onion
- 2 clove garlic
- Caper Salsa Verde
- 1/4 cup of fresh parsley
- 1/4 cup of fresh basil
- 1 green onion
- 1/4 cup of extra-virgin olive oil
- 2 tbsp. capers
- 1 1/2 tbsp fresh lemon juice

1. Preheat the oven to 425 degrees Fahrenheit. In a 12-inch cast-iron pan, bring the broth to a boil. Pour the liquid over the couscous in a medium bowl, then cover and leave aside.
2. Now warm the oil in a pan over medium-high heat until it is quite hot. Season the chicken with salt and pepper before serving. Place the chicken skin side down in a pan and cook for 10 minutes, or until the skin is browned and crispy. Then cook for another 4 minutes on the other side. Remove the chicken to a platter and remove the drippings.
3. Sauté peppers and following 2 ingredients 3 minutes. Place skin-side up chicken on top of peppers. Preheat oven to 425° Fahrenheit and bake for 10 minutes, or until done.
4. Mix couscous with a fork. Serve the chicken and peppers over couscous and sprinkle with as much salsa as desired.
5. Combine parsley, basil, green onion, olive oil, capers, and lemon juice in a bowl. Season with salt and pepper to taste.

Prep Time: 20 Mins

Bake Time: 55 Mins

Total Time: 1 Hr 15 Mins

Servings: 12

INGREDIENTS

- 6 cups of crumbled cornbread
- 2 cups of white bread cubes, toasted
- 1 cup of chopped pecans
- 1/4 cup of minced fresh parsley
- 1 tsp dried thyme
- 1/2 tsp rubbed sage
- 1/2 tsp salt
- 1/2 tsp pepper
- 1 pound bulk pork sausage
- 2 tbsp butter
- 2 large tart apples, diced
- 1 cup of diced celery
- 1 medium onion, finely chopped
- 1-3/4 to 2-1/4 cups of chicken broth

1. Combine the bread, pecans, and spices in a large bowl; put aside. Now crumble the sausage and fry it in a big pan made of cast iron or another pan that can go in the oven until it is no longer pink, doing so while breaking it up into crumbs. Drain on paper towels after removing with slotted spoon.
2. Toss in the apples, celery, and onion with the drippings and cook until soft. Stir in the sausage and just enough liquid to moisten the bread mixture.
3. Fill a cast-iron pan halfway with the ingredients; cover and bake at 350° for 45 minutes. Uncover and bake for ten minutes, or until just set.

Prep Time: 20 Mins

Cook Time: 10 Mins

Total Time: 30 Mins

Servings: 4

INGREDIENTS

- 6 large eggs
- 1 tsp kosher salt
- 1/2 tsp freshly ground pepper
- 2 cups of 1/2- to 3/4-inch-cubed sweet potatoes
- 2 tbsp. olive oil, divided
- 2 cups of firmly packed chopped kale
- 1/2 small chopped red onion
- 2 minced garlic cloves
- 3-ounce goat crumbled cheese

INSTRUCTIONS

1. Preheat the oven to 350 degrees Fahrenheit. Combine the eggs and the following three ingredients in a bowl.

2. In a 10-inch ovenproof nonstick pan, sauté sweet potatoes in 1 tbsp hot oil for 8-10 minutes, or until tender and golden brown. Remove and keep warm. In the remaining 1 tbsp of oil, sauté kale and the next 2 ingredients 3-4 minutes, or until kale is wilted and tender; mix in potatoes. Cook for another 3 minutes after pouring the egg mixture equally over the veggies. Goat cheese should be sprinkled over the egg mixture.
3. Bake for 10 to 14 minutes at 350°F, or until set.

MUENSTER BREAD

Prep Time: 20 Mins

Bake Time: 40 Mins

Total Time: 1 Hr

Servings: 16

INGREDIENTS

- 2 packets active dry yeast (1/4 ounce each)
- 1 cup of warm 2% milk
- 1/2 cup of softened butter
- 2 tbsp sugar
- 1 tsp salt
- 3-1/4 to 3-3/4 cups of all-purpose flour
- 1 large egg yolk and 1 large egg, room temperature
- 4 cups of shredded Muenster cheese
- 1 large egg white, beaten

INSTRUCTIONS

1. First, dissolve yeast in milk in a large bowl. Combine the butter, sugar, salt, and 2 cups flour and beat until smooth. Then, using the remaining flour, create a soft dough.
2. Now knead for 6-8 minutes on a floured surface until smooth and elastic. In an oiled bowl, flip the top to coat with oil. Allow to rise for approximately one hour in a warm place, until it has doubled in size.
3. Mix the egg and yolk in a large bowl; stir in the cheese. Roll the dough into a 16-inch circle after punching it down.
4. Allow dough to drape over the rims of a greased 10-inch cast-iron skillet or 9-inch round baking pan. Spoon the cheese mixture into the dough's middle. Make 1-1/2-inch pleats in the dough over the filling. To construct a topknot, gently squeeze the pleats together at the top and twist. Allow for a 10–15-minutes rise time.
5. Brush the egg white on the loaf. Preheat oven to 375° Fahrenheit and bake for 40-45 minutes. Allow to cool for 20 minutes on a wire rack. Serve immediately.

SEARED GROUPER WITH CORN, ZUCCHINI, AND TOMATO SAUTÉ

Total Time: 20 Mins

Servings: 4

INGREDIENTS

- 4 grouper fillets, or other firm fish
- 1 tsp kosher salt
- 1/2 tsp Freshly ground pepper
- 2 tbsp olive oil
- 2 medium zucchini, halved lengthwise and sliced
- 1 large, chopped shallot
- 1 1/2 cups of fresh yellow corn kernels
- 2 minced garlic cloves
- 1 1/2 cups of halved cherry tomatoes
- 2 tbsp cubed cold butter
- 1/4 cup of torn basil leaves

INSTRUCTIONS

1. Add salt and pepper to the fish. Then warm the oil in a large nonstick skillet by keeping the heat at medium-high. Cook the fish for 4 minutes on each side, or until golden brown and cooked through. Remove from the oven and keep warm.

2. Sauté zucchini and shallot for 4 minutes, or until crisp-tender. Sauté for another 2 minutes after adding the corn and garlic. After that, decrease the heat to low and add the tomatoes, butter, and basil, stirring constantly until the butter is melted. To taste, season with salt and pepper. Place the veggies on serving dishes, then top with the fish.